The Sunken Quest,
the Wasted Fisher,
the Pregnant Fish

The Sunken Quest, the Wasted Fisher, the Pregnant Fish

Postmodern Reflections on Depth Psychology

Ronald Schenk

Chiron Publications
Wilmette, Illinois

Library of Congress Catalog Card Number: 2001001036

Library of Congress Cataloging-in-Publication Data:

Schenk, Ronald, 1944–
The sunken quest, the wasted fisher, the pregnant fish : postmodern reflections on
    depth psychology / Ronald Schenk.
        p.   cm.
    Includes bibliographical references and index.
    ISBN 1-888602-15-5 (alk. paper)
    1. Psychoanalysis.   2. Jungian psychology.   3. Jung, C. G. (Carl Gustav),
1875-1961. I. Title.
    BF173.S33 2001
    150.19'54—dc21   2001001036

Printed in the United States of America.
Cover design by D. J. Hyde.

To Herb, Ray, Joan, and Rhoda

We are caught and entangled in aimless experience, and the judging intellect with its categories proves itself powerless. Human interpretation fails, for a turbulent life-situation has arisen that refuses to fit any of the traditional meanings assigned to it. It is a moment of collapse. We sink into a final depth—Apuleius calls it "a kind of voluntary death." It is a surrender of our own powers, not artificially willed but forced upon us by nature; not a voluntary submission and humiliation decked in moral garb but an utter and unmistakable defeat crowned with the panic fear of demoralization. Only when all props and crutches are broken, and no cover from the rear offers even the slightest hope of security, does it become possible for us to experience an archetype that up till then had lain hidden to experience.

—Jung, *Archetypes and the Collective Unconscious*

Going to a dark bed there was a square round Sinbad the Sailor roc's auk's egg in the night of the bed of all the auks of the rocs of Darkinbad the Brightdayler.

—Joyce, *Ulysses*

Hesiod is the teacher of very many, he who did not understand day and night: for they are one.

—Heraclitus

CONTENTS

PREFACE

Decentering the Soul

Although Sigmund Freud and C. G. Jung heroically pioneered the foundation and practice of a psychology of the unconscious or depth psychology, their roots in rationalism kept them from seeing and giving expression to the full relativizing possibilities of their vision. As a result, practitioners of both Freudian and Jungian psychoanalysis have maintained a predominately rational approach to the irrationality of unconscious life. This book is a collection of essays articulating a vision of depth psychology, particularly influenced by Jung, that emphasizes a postmodern sensibility toward psychological life from the decentered perspective articulated in such postmodern orientations as phenomenology, deconstruction, quantum physics, chaos theory, and aesthetics, which is inherent in Jung's psychology.

Like all psychological formulations, what is postmodern is an attitude of mind that can't be solidified in definition but does reflect several characteristic qualities. With postmodern sensibility, language and image envelop authorship; ego is undermined. A text appears in which nouns as fixity are less important than the fluidity of verbs and adverbs. Tone becomes more ironic than triumphant. With singularity of vision dissolved, multiplicities of perspective bubble up and hierarchy tumbles. Cause loses its privilege, and no one point of origination can hold its place. Whereas modernity strives nostalgically toward an unpresentable source, the postmodern looks to the structure of signifiers at hand or to the gap between sign and source. On the other hand, postmodern consciousness comes about not in isolation, but always in relation to an other; the postmodern itself is always bouncing off modernity.

Postmodern is an attitude that inclines toward interval—between I and not-I, body and world, forming and being formed. Shaken by context, facts are dissolved by questions, meaning flits about, eluding categories, and words cannot escape the relativization of quotation marks. Deprived of consolation of alignment with authority, consciousness is freed up to play in carnivalesque event. Understanding becomes unfixed, a matter of allusion, sand play, as interpretation caves in on itself. The center has not only lost its hold, the whole undone, but the very limits of circumference have been brought to disperse amidst the shakeup. This book is an attempt to clarify how these themes reveal themselves in depth psychology.

The first four chapters lay out the argument. "Myths of Meaning" shows two fundamental worlds of understanding contained in Jung's thought—traditional nineteenth-century rationalism and postmodern aesthetic—each housing its own set of assumptions, language, and orientation, with the latter lending itself to a truly psychological vision. "The Body in Analysis" then gives a vision of the conjunction of body/mind/world in the image of disease. "A Ground for Psyche" furthers the elaboration of the themes of the first two chapters and shows how phenomenology as a psychology of experience reveals Jung's thought to be subtly grounded in the immediacy of experience as opposed to the metapsychology that structures most traditional Jungian thinking. "The Temple of Dionysus" presents a view of dream life as religious event.

The last four chapters move more into the imaginal realm. "Shipwrecks and Dicethrows" provides images for a deconstructive approach to psychological life. "Psyche Re-membered" proposes that while Jung's personal blind spots led to a serious lack in his most commonly expressed theory and practice, alchemy and chaos theory help us to see that the integration of personal and universal that he sought is subtly achieved in his work. "Mining/Fishing/Analysis" weaves strands from alchemy, literature, and analytic thought to form a vision of analysis based on seduction. Finally, "The Sunken Quest/The Wasted Fisher/The Pregnant Fish" uses Eliot's poem, *The Waste Land,* as a model for a contemporary psychoanalysis.

ACKNOWLEDGMENTS

The guiding light of this book is C. G. Jung, and my writing is an attempt to meet his thought. James Hillman has carried the torch of Jung's postmodern spirit, especially in his sense of image. David Miller has been a continuous inspiration for paradoxical thinking. Patricia Berry, Edward Casey, Paul Kugler, and Roger Brooke have all preceded me in their writing, and I am grateful for their influence.

Some of the chapters in this book were first presented as papers at various Jungian conferences, and my gratitude goes to the following organizers and organizations: Murray Stein and Nathan Schwartz-Salant, Chiron Conference, 1984, "The Body in Analysis"; the Inter-Regional Society of Jungian Analysts, 1984, "The Fool in Depth Psychology"; the C. G. Jung Institute of Dallas Conference, 1992, "Following the Spirit: Jung in an Age of Uncertainty"; Stan Marlan, the Inter-Regional Society of Jungian Analysts Conference, 1993, "Alchemy and Seduction"; the Jung Society of New York, The National Conference of Jungian Analysts, 1997, "Jung and Postmodernism"; James Hollis, the C. G. Jung Educational Center of Houston, 1998, "Remembering Psyche."

I am grateful for the courage of my patient, "M" of chapter 8, in the therapeutic endeavor and for his support of this project.

I am indebted to Siobhan Drummond for her masterful work in editing the various versions of my manuscript and to Murray Stein for his help in bringing the book into publication.

Finally, I give thanks to my wife, Charlotte, for her love during the years of this book's emergence.

Permission is gratefully acknowledged for the following:

An earlier version of chapter 1, "Myths of Meaning," was published in *Spring* 56 (Fall 1994).

An earlier version of chapter 2, "The Body in Analysis: Bare Bones—The Aesthetics of Arthritis," was published as "Bare Bones: The Aesthetics of Arthritis" by Chiron Publications in *The Body in Analysis*, edited by Nathan Schwartz-Salant and Murray Stein, 1986.

An earlier version of chapter 3, "A Ground for Psyche," was published as "A Ground for Jungian Thought" by *The San Francisco Jung Institute Library Journal*, volume 11, number 3, 1992.

An earlier version of chapter 4, "The Temple of Dionysus: Dreams as Religious Experience," was published as "The Dream as Religious Experience" in *The Journal of Pastoral Counseling*, volume 26, 1991.

An earlier version of chapter 7, "Mining/Fishing/Analysis: Seduction as Alchemical *Extractio*," was published by Chiron Publications in *Fire in the Stone: The Alchemy of Desire*, edited and introduced by Stanton Marlan, 1997.

Jung, Carl Gustav, *The Collected Works of C. G. Jung.* Copyright © 1977 by Princeton University Press. Reprinted by permission of Princeton University Press.

From COLLECTED POEMS by Wallace Stevens. Copyright 1942 by Wallace Stevens and renewed 1970 by Holly Stevens. Reprinted by permission of Alfred A. Knopf, a division of Random House, Inc. Further permission gratefully acknowledged from Faber and Faber Ltd.

For selections and excerpts from "Lace Passes into Nothingness . . .," "Will New and Alive The Beautiful Today," and "The Windows" by Stéphane Mallarmé, from SELECTED POETRY AND PROSE, copyright ©1982 by New Directions Publishing Corp. Reprinted by permission of New Directions Publishing Corp.

For the excerpt from "Dice Thrown Never will Annul Chance" by Stéphane Mallarmé, Mary Ann Caws, from SELECTED POETRY AND PROSE, copyright ©1982 by Mary Ann Caws. Reprinted by permission of New Directions Publishing Corp.

1

MYTHS OF MEANING

Jung's work can be seen against a backdrop of many different periods of history as well as genres. At different times, he seems Homeric, Heraclitean, Platonic, early Christian, medieval alchemical, Renaissance, Neoplatonic, seventeenth-century rationalist, eighteenth-century romantic, and nineteenth-century scientistic as well as twentieth-century postmodern. On different occasions, he writes like an experimental scientist, a criminal detective, a medical doctor, a religious mystic, a mythographer, a philosopher of history, a historian of religion, a social moralist, an alchemist, an archeologist, or a psychotherapeutic clinician. His different backgrounds reflect different assumptions and preconceptions regarding experience, perception, and meaning, in short, a different mode of being, a different world. This diversity of ontological positions bespeaks the mercurial nature of both Jung and the psyche itself, which can never be reflected in one mirror. When we read Jung, we are always forced to be careful to examine the underlying preconceptions and suppositions, that is, the ground of being of any one book, lecture, paragraph, sentence, or even phrase.

Although Jung covers many ontologies, time and again he says directly or indirectly that his work is in the service of one intention—to reveal the reality of psychic life (1956, p. 156; 1959, p. 48; 1966b, p. 95; 1968a, p. 116; 1969a, pp. 247, 359; 1969b, p. 354; 1971, pp. 41, 52). Intrinsic to his notion of the reality of the psyche was his faith in "meaning." Life is not merely the accumulation of experience, but, more importantly, the carrier of meaningful intention as well. Exactly what he understood as meaning is the subject of this chapter.

I would like to explore the implications of two paradigms of Jung's project. The first emerges out of modern, rationalist, subjectivist ground, which finds meaning by detaching observer and observed, splitting psyche and world, and foisting abstract categories and conceptual grids onto experience. The second I am calling a postmodern paradigm, which paradoxically comes out of a long historical tradition. It states that we live *in* psychic image and that image holds meaning in and of itself.

Jung recognized that the effort to find meaning inevitably leads to a tension—the urge to find meaning is countered by the realization that we are always experiencing life, including the life of psychological inquiry, *through* facts that encompass our conscious experience. The phenomenologist Maurice Merleau-Ponty expressed it this way:

> [W]e cannot subject our perception of the world to philosophical scrutiny without ceasing to be identified with that act of positing the world, with that interest in it which delimits us, without drawing back from our commitment which is itself thus made to appear as a spectacle, without passing from the *fact* of our existence to its *nature*, from the Dasein to the Wesen. (1962, p. xiv)

These facts that are being lived through us are not only concealed personal inclinations, which Michael Polanyi (1958) referred to as "personal knowledge" and Jung calls "complexes," but universal patterns, images, and modes which Jung calls "archetypal" and which are ultimately beyond our ability to know. Jung wrote, "The psyche . . . observes itself and can only translate the psychic back into the psychic" (1969b, p. 216). The psyche is both the object and the subject of psychology. While we are trying to apprehend a certainty of meaning in experience, at the same time the very means through which we are experiencing that endeavor renders our attempts uncertain. We can never rest in our experience of ourselves as subjects, yet our being as object of an other is beyond our comprehension. Jung makes this dilemma clear in a story from his childhood. As a boy sitting on a stone, he wondered whether he was the boy on the stone, or the stone imagining a boy sitting on him (1961, p. 20). This tension is at the heart of Jung's endeavor to honor psychic reality, as he slides back and

forth between the subjective certainty of modernism and the uncertainty of postmodernism.

It is important to read Jung with an eye that sees through
his language and reflects upon the adequacy of his ontological
ground at any one point in revealing the full complexity and paradoxical nature of psychological life. My contention will be that
when he is in the modernist mode of deriving meaning through
conceptual systems, Jung remains trapped in a world that does not
allow him to honor experience in its most complete sense, that is,
by sensing the meaning inherent in experience itself. When he is in
the postmodern paradigm of imagination, Jung senses the poetic
nature of the psyche and comes closer to his intention of honoring
psychic life.

The Modern Paradigm of Meaning

Jung lived and worked, especially in the first half of his life, at a
time when the values of modernity were at their zenith. Reality was
that which could be seen and measured as repeatable by the objective eye following the rationalist ontology of Descartes and New-
ton. The universe was conceived in terms of absolute time and
space, matter was considered as qualitatively separate from energy,
material objects were thought to interact with each other according
to quantitative relations, and the universe was imagined as operating like a machine in a deterministic, cause–effect manner. Subjective consciousness was primary, a consciousness which imputes life
exclusively to interior being and forces a split between that which
is seen as material and that which is thought to be mind. In this
world, spirit was consigned to institutionalized religion or transcen-
dental philosophies, while body was lost completely (until resur-
rected in the hysterical bodies of the early patients of
psychoanalysis). At the same time, the collective ethos was one of
detached observing, exploring, consuming, and controlling the
world as dead. Its premodern cultures were treated as objects in
the service of a self-certain, subjective "I." For T. S. Eliot, modern
life was a half-life lived among a "heap of broken images," and for
Jung, modern man was "in search of a soul."

Jung nonetheless struggled to find alternatives to the modernist mode of being and finding meaning. On the one hand, he

sought to displace rationalism as the sole means for achieving meaning, to supplant materialism and positivism as the dominant way of seeing, and to undermine subjectivism as the sovereign ground of being. On the other hand, he tried to reveal a different reality, the reality of the psyche, which included material and spiritual being that ultimately exist paradoxically in each other. Yet, ironically, in this effort Jung often used the language of subjectivism and rationalism, in effect, stood on the very ground he was trying to undermine. From this stance, Jung viewed the psyche through a dualistic, Cartesian lens, using abstract concepts such as "conscious," "unconscious," "complex," "archetype," "masculine," "feminine," and "self." He emphasized the interiority of psyche, splitting it from the world seen as outside the individual. He characterized the psyche as having "contents" invoking a dualistic observer/observed model. He imagined "the dynamics of the psyche" in terms of quantitative energetic laws from nineteenth-century thermodynamics and hydraulics (Jung 1969b, pp. 25ff, 38ff) and employed mechanistic systems of interpretation. He spoke of psychic movement as a "journey," the unconscious as "territory" to be explored, and of the world of people and things as something that was "projected" upon (ibid., p. 264), evoking metaphors which reinforced a heroic, dualistic, ego-based consciousness.

Because Jungians have generally tended to follow Jung in his rationalist mode, thereby erecting a fortress of conceptual structures around the psyche, it is important to investigate some of the sources of this mode and their implications. Jung wrote several papers following his book, *Symbols of Transformation* (1956), to further differentiate his thought from psychoanalysis. In "On Psychic Energy" (1969b), Jung wanted to show that the psyche was a dynamic system of values based on quantities of energy, rather than simply a materialistic, causal mechanism. He stated that depression, as well as being caused by something such as the regression of instinctual energy, could also take place for a purpose. The purposive or finalistic nature of depression was its ability to evoke associations by means of which further development could take place.

> What the regression brings to the surface certainly seems at first sight to be slime from the depths; but if one does not stop short at a superficial evaluation and refrains from passing judgement on

the basis of a preconceived dogma, it will be found that this "slime" contains not merely incompatible and rejected remnants of everyday life, or inconvenient and objectionable animal tendencies, but also germs of new life and vital possibilities for the future. (Ibid., pp. 34–35)

In other words, Jung wanted to show that, as well as being *caused* by a source, our being *intends* toward something greater than we can know.

In order to make his point, Jung fit his ideas into a nineteenth-century model of thermodynamics, heavily influenced by Newtonian physics, featuring two major laws. The first law of thermodynamics states that the total energy involved in a process is always conserved. The second law states that processes proceed from order to disorder until there is a *balance* of energy. Jung described the psyche through these models from classical physics as a closed system in which "libido" or "life-energy" operated between pairs of mutually exclusive aspects, which he termed "opposites" (Jung 1969b, pp. 17, 26). When the energetic value of one aspect is increased, it draws on the energy of its opposite. Psychological energy consciously invested in an "outer world" (seen as split from psyche) calls for energy to be drawn to "inner life" (ibid., p. 39).

Following Newtonian physics, the sum of the two mutually exclusive parts equals the whole. The unconscious aspect of the psyche draws energy from an overly developed conscious aspect. Jung saw the overall need of the psyche (what he called "wholeness" or "totality") as being served by the "self-regulating" aspect of the psyche (Jung 1966b, p. 61; 1969b, p. 79), that is, the tendency toward *balancing* two separate and opposing aspects of the same system. In this system, psyche is located in "inner" life. Just as for Descartes, the only thing that could be determined as real was the fact of consciousness as "inner," so for Jung, in this paradigm, what is experienced as "outer" is a matter of projection of unconscious contents. What Jung called "wholeness" becomes a matter of making conscious the unconscious (1969b, p. 79) by withdrawing projections. One takes back the projection through the awareness that what is seen as outside oneself is actually an unconscious aspect of oneself. The Jung of this paradigm wrote,

All the contents of our unconscious are constantly being projected
into our surroundings, and it is only by recognizing certain properties of the object as projections . . . that we are able to distinguish them from the real properties of the objects. (Ibid., p. 264)

In short, the world of people and things is separate from, projected
upon, and affecting a psyche encased in body. Jung moves away
from a Cartesian/Freudian world in gaining the sense of a purposive process in the psyche, but he remains in the Cartesian world of
split perception. Psyche is still encapsulated in a body, existing in a
dead world.

To be sure, Jung does allow that projections take place
when there is a "hook" outside oneself (1969b, p. 53), that is, an
objective reality to perception, but for the most part, Jung and Jungians have used the notion of projection from a Cartesian standpoint. Jung also proposes a connection between psyche and world,
the results of which he puts into a special category of events he
termed "synchronicity." The concept of synchronicity suggests there
is a mysterious principle at work in the universe, transcending
Newtonian notions of space and time, by which two meaningfully
but not causally related events occur simultaneously (ibid., p. 441).
However, the image of the hook and the idea of synchronicity only
make sense to a mind that has already split psyche and world.

A related aspect of Jung's concept of oppositions, based on
the second law of thermodynamics from classical physics, is his
system of interpretation through compensation. Jung's hydraulics
paradigm for the psyche views energy quantitatively (Jung 1969b,
pp. 38–39). So unconscious life expressed in dreams serves a compensatory function for conscious life. If my dreams are dark, it is
compensation for my overly bright conscious attitude.

If we want to interpret a dream correctly, we need a thorough
knowledge of the conscious situation at that moment, because the
dream contains its unconscious complement, that is, the material
which the conscious situation has constellated in the unconscious.
(Ibid., pp. 248–9)

Jung's system of interpretation through compensation rests
on the idea that the sum of the parts equals the whole and that energy flows from an overly emphasized aspect to the opposite, un-

deremphasized part in an attempt to bring order to the system. Interpretation is accomplished through the conscious attitude of the dreamer, which doesn't appear in the dream itself. Consciousness and unconsciousness are different sides of a system that seeks balance and harmony. One cannot analyze a dream image without measuring it against a conscious association that might not have anything to do with the actual dream experience. The result, as James Hillman (1979b) has pointed out, is that the analyst is put in a position of moral authority. The dreamer needs to change his or her attitude according to the analyst's interpretation. The system of interpretation takes precedence over the experience of the dream.

Jung's rationalistic view of psychic structure, as well as dynamics, is based upon an ideal of balance. Through the system of typology, meaning is derived by an Aristotelian categorizing of personalities into types. Individuals can be divided into two basic categories based on a split between inner and outer, namely, introverted and extraverted. Two subcategories split perception from judgment, each with opposing polarities that separate sensing and intuiting on the one hand and thinking and feeling on the other. Again, there are dualisms, as though my "inner life"—memory, for example—were not intricately connected with the things of the world, or as though my thinking and feeling did not inherently coconstitute each other. What holds meaning is not the actual experience itself but the system from which it is derived.

Jung's notions of "individuation" and "self" also suffer from the dangers of conceptual, abstract, and subjective interpretation. At times, Jung conceives of individuation, the process through which the personality unfolds toward a goal that is at once personal and transcendent, from a Cartesian standpoint. Individuation is an "inner," solitary "journey," separate from the "outer" world (Jung 1969b, pp. 36–7). Jung described the concept of the self in terms denoting centrality (1966b, pp. 221, 238; 1968a, p. 181; 1969a, p. 41), totality (1959, pp. 62, 268; 1968a, p. 142; 1969a, pp. 41, 82), unity (1959, p. 268; 1968b, p. 25; 1969b, p. 199), wholeness (1956, p. 303; 1968a, p. 164; 1969a, p. 582), and goal of life (1966b, pp. 239, 240; 1969a, p. 582), all of which refer meaning to an omnipotent, abstract authority. This authority deprives the lived experiential world of meaning.

All of these systems, resting on notions of balance,

harmony, and order, have their roots in the classical conceptual system of proportion. In proportion, concrete particularity is reducible to unity through order in the relationship of the parts. Perception through proportion refers to a transcendent authority, the unity of the whole and, in particular, its center at the expense of the part, the fragment, which is our actual experience.

Proportional perception works against the honoring of experience. The eye anchored in proportion loses the concrete for the abstract. One of its earliest elaborators, Pythagoras, saw things as numbers and the contemplation of numbers as a means of transcending the physical world. The imposition of numerical order on experience gives the observer a sense of control but loses the particularity of the experience. The emphasis on a center gives rise to a unitary, monotheistic consciousness that is comforting to the ego because it is in alignment with a fixed, divine source but misses the flux of the world. (Pythagoras would try to fix the world with numbers, but Heraclitus said you could not enter the same river twice.)

Finally, rationalist concepts and systems presuppose an ontology of observer split off from observed. Perception is through the detached eye of the observer. That which is "other," whether the "contents" of an unconscious "inner world" (Jung 1969b, pp. 11, 139, 151, 165) or objective "outer" world, is described and organized to enhance the self-certainty of subjective consciousness.

All of the ways we have seen so far from which Jung derives meaning—rationalism, classical physics, and proportion—serve to enhance subjectivism. Yet, an alternative paradigm, which I would like to characterize as postmodern, was also working through Jung in a subtler way.

The Postmodern Paradigm of Meaning

The term *postmodern* ironically hearkens back to a long tradition of imagination, and while it reacts against modern rationalism, it therefore depends on it. It de-centers, de-subjectivizes, or deconstructs experience so that a sense of an "other" emerges. This other has a life of its own which encompasses subjective experience. Jung referred to the other in several ways—"unconscious," "soul," "*anthropos*," "original man," "shadow," "anima," "animus," "self," etc.

Postmodernism is pervaded with a mood of uncertainty. Paul Kugler (1987, p. 54) tells the story of Mullah, a character from a series of ancient Persian stories, who rides by his friends several times on a horse as though looking for something. When they finally ask him what he is doing, he says he is looking for his horse. We can never find what is riding us, driving us, moving us, because it is itself the very means of the search. Answers to questions about the nature of the universe depend on the point of view of the questioner.

The dynamic of postmodernism is one of play. Consciousness is always bouncing back and forth, to and fro between perspectives—boy or stone, self or other, wave or particle, subject or object—in a hermeneutic circle. We have an idea and then realize that it has us. This play can take on an erotic tone, as in a tennis match with its love scores where the back and forth of the ball keeps the players directly connected to each other. It can also take on a deadly aspect, as in the earnest play to the death of ancient Mayan ballplayers.

Play makes itself known through the display of pattern. For the philosopher Plotinus, beauty is the force in the universe that allows for the appearance of things, events, and images, each having a perfection of its own. Theoreticians of mathematics look to the beauty of patterns of numbers on computer printouts while psychotherapists see an entity in the depression or anger or contempt of their patients (Schwartz-Salant 1989, pp. 131ff).

Jung and Postmodernism

While Jung's rationalist stance separates observer from observed in the Cartesian-Newtonian tradition, postmodern physics says that the world takes on different qualities depending on the questions asked of it. In subatomic physics, there is a dual aspect to both matter and light, that is, a particle quality and a wave quality. Matter or light at any one time will act like a wave or a particle according to the type of inquiry. The more I know of the world from the standpoint of particles, the less I will know of its wave nature and vice versa. What we see is not nature itself, but that particular aspect of nature that is exposed to our questioning.

Observer and observed form a gestalt, that is, the whole is

greater than the sum of the parts. Here, the world is not a closed energy system. Instead, the particle world and the wave world are qualitatively different and mutually exclusive. We are left in uncertainty, and, as Heisenberg formulated, we can only find meaning in probabilities (the superposition encompassing both waves and particles). The movement toward wholeness here is not a cumulative process but a transformation to a qualitatively different plane.

In sum, quantum physics takes us out of the positivist shadows of Jung's systems of typology and ego-self and render obsolete the observer-observed model of the psyche, the notion of compensation based on a quantitative, self-enclosed energy system and the preconception that harmony is a goal of natural systems. As we shall see in chapter 6, contemporary chaos theory asserts that systems do not seek homeostasis, balance, harmony, or order, but rather a condition that allows for a multiplicity of potentials for furthering the process, or as Jung said, "Man needs difficulties; they are necessary for health" (1969b, p. 73).

While Jung's rationalist mode takes us away from experience in order to derive meaning, phenomenology helps us to see a side of Jung that emphasizes experience rather than concept as the ground of meaning. Phenomenology distrusts all rational impositions onto experience. The Jung of this second paradigm shares in this distrust, favoring instead contact with the world over science, actual experience over theory, mutual reflection with the patient over objective understanding (1964, p. 250; 1966a, pp. 145–6; 1966b, pp. 246–7). Likewise, regarding typology, this Jung cautions:

> [F]ar too many readers have succumbed to the error of thinking that . . . ("General Description of Types") . . . provides a system of classification and a practical guide to a good judgment of human character . . . . This regrettable misunderstanding completely ignores the fact that this kind of classification is nothing but a childish parlour game. (1971, p. xiv)

In the same anticonceptual vein, Jung wrote regarding the self and individuation:

> The *idiosyncrasy* of an individual is . . . to be understood as . . . a *unique* combination, or gradual differentiation, of functions and

faculties which in themselves are universal . . . . Individuation, therefore, can only mean a process of psychological development that fulfills the *individual* qualities given . . . it is a process by which a man becomes the definite, unique being he in fact is . . . fulfilling the *peculiarity* of his nature. (1966b, pp. 173–4, italics added)

"As the apotheosis of *individuality,* the self has the attributes of *uniqueness* and of occurring once only in time" (Jung 1959, p. 62, italics added). In this mode, we see the phenomenological Jung undermining the abstract authority imputed to conceptual systems. Here, it is experience in the world, the unique perception of the individual, and the oddity of personality that elicit meaning.

Phenomenology seeks to reveal the essence of experience. Jung was phenomenological in that he understood the psyche through its own language: myth, fairy tale, religious symbol, alchemy, bodily symptoms, love affairs, and pathological behavior. It was in the aberrant and irrational expressions of life itself that Jung saw the essence of psyche at work and found meaning. It is this Jung that wrote, "the psyche is indistinguishable from its manifestations" (1969a, p. 49).

In phenomenology, consciousness is always consciousness *of* something. There is always an intentionality *toward* something; no dualism exists between mind and world. It is not that the psyche functions as an interior mechanism in a world that affects it, but that the lived world is "gathered" as psyche exists. In this light, Jung saw the world as though for the first time on his trip to Africa (Brooke 1991, p. 60). He wrote of standing on the plains of Uganda, where

> Grazing, heads nodding, the herds moved forward like slow rivers. There was scarcely any sound save the melancholy cry of a bird of prey. This was the stillness of the eternal beginning, the world as it had always been, in the state of non-being; for until then no-one had been present to know that it was this world. (1961, p. 255)

Individuation here is not just communion with something innermost but an openness to worldly being wherein inner and outer are in mutual coexistence. Elsewhere, Jung wrote,

> Widened consciousness . . . is a function of relationship to the
> world of objects, bringing the individual into absolute, binding,
> and indissoluble communion with the world at large. (1966b,
> p. 178)

Jung furthered his understanding of the connection between psyche and world when he pointed out that "projections are
always there first and are recognized afterwards" (1968a, p. 61). In
other words, it is only when we doubt our experience in the same
way as Descartes that we can even talk in terms of projections. Projections are never "taken back" really; they are simply moved on to
another place or replaced by another projection. We are always in
a projective connection with the world. Meaning becomes not so
much a matter of extracting spirit from world by taking back projections but the recognition of the coconstitution of world and
psyche.

Jung wrote that the principle of synchronicity indicated a
"general acausal orderedness" (1969b, p. 516). In other words, a
meaningful connection between events in which one does not
cause the other is *not* exceptional; rather, it follows a general principle.[1] "Psyche and matter exist in one and the same world, and
each partakes of the other" (Jung 1959, p. 261). "Psyche is simply
'world'" (Jung 1968a, p. 173).

From the phenomenological standpoint, the distinction between conscious and unconscious is not as clean as Jung, the rationalist "making conscious the unconscious," would have it.
Consciousness is a state constantly interpenetrated by unconsciousness. In the language of phenomenology, openness is always permeated by a closed quality of being, revealing clouded with
concealing. Jung, the phenomenologist, said:

> [W]e come to the paradoxical conclusion that there is no con-
> scious content which is not in some other respect unconscious.
> Maybe, too, there is no unconscious psychism that is not at the
> same time conscious. (1969b, p. 188)

This attitude allows us to look not just to dreams, but to everyday
life, as Freud did, to see the unconscious working through us in
slips of the tongue, changes of mood, and the sounds of our everyday language. The unconscious now becomes an everyday absence

that is present in its own terms, its own rhythms, its own images—an incarnate necessity which stretches from the past, remains in the present, intends a future, and calls for appropriation and reflection. In sum, from the standpoint of phenomenology and the phenomenological Jung, the psyche is both within and without. To use an image from the Renaissance to which Jung often referred, the psyche is like a sphere wherein the center is nowhere and the circumference everywhere.

Alchemy is a third model revealing postmodern sensibility, and during the latter third of his career, Jung turned to alchemy for metaphors of psychological life. Alchemy is postmodern in its imagistic nature, which serves to de-center consciousness. It provides rich, concrete images of precisely detailed codes, recipes, parables, and stories, expressing a multitude of distinct psychological situations all regarded as natural conditions in which the soul finds itself. Each condition is a visible world or metaphor of habitation with its own particular images, colors, metals, animals, feeling tones, and behavior patterns. Each world has its own center and is considered in itself a goal as well as a beginning.

Alchemy sees process in natural movements from one condition to another, rather than in invisible energies. The attainment of the black, depressed condition is paradoxically seen as an achievement because the workings of natural life can be considered a series of deaths (Waite 1976, p. 9). The alchemical sense of process is postmodern in that it works upon the practitioner as well as the matter, dissolving the split between subject and object.

In alchemy, what Jung categorizes as opposites are instead referred to as distinct qualities such as the wet and the dry, the lower and the higher, the vulgar and the sacred, the fixed and the volatile, which paradoxically fit with each other and reflect a sense of paradox in experience. "Our water is our fire." The stone, the metaphor for the goal of the work, is at the same time not a stone. It is visible to all eyes, yet unknown. Black and white are not opposites but related conditions of different quality. The alchemical process can move back and forth between the two qualities, now emphasizing one, now the other.

Finally, alchemy attributes life or subjectivity to what we think of as dead matter. In alchemy, all matter contains seeds from the different planets, each of which has a distinct quality of life.

This life in matter is presented in distinct personalities like Mercurius, Mars, Saturn, and Venus.

In a statement that serves as a summary of his postmodern stance, Jung writes:

> [C]onscious and unconscious are not necessarily in opposition to one another, but complement one another to form a totality . . . that is supraordinate to the conscious ego. It . . . is therefore . . . a personality which we *also* are. (1966b, p. 177)

Here he is at once in the mind of phenomenology, which emphasizes the meaning inherent in experience, of quantum physics, which finds a supraordinate realm encompassing two complementary realms, and of alchemy in giving personality to this "other" realm or mode.

Postmodern as Aesthetic

Jung characterized this alternative, irrational paradigm—what I am referring to as "postmodern"—as *esse in anima* or being in soul, and he founded it on aesthetics or image (1971, pp. 51–2; Berry 1983). The germinating seeds for this paradigm can be seen relatively early in his career when he struggled with the notion that meaning and form are opposites, corresponding to what he saw as the opposition of conscious and unconscious. In his struggle, he said,

> The ideal case would be if these two aspects could exist side by side or rhythmically succeed each other; that is if there were an alternation of creation and understanding. (1969b, p. 86)

Jung could see that our experience wants both shape and meaning, and he saw the weaving together of the two in the symbolic image. Jung is careful to say that the symbol is not the sum of two parts, but a qualitatively different experience, a "new level of being, a new situation," a "newly won attitude" (ibid., pp. 90, 72–3). He called this process the "transcendent function." Although his rational language forced him to use the concept of opposites coming together, the idea of the symbol as the best expression of that which can't be expressed allows for two qualitatively different aspects to be already existing in each other. The notion of the symbol, then, is one step out of a dualistic vision and toward an imaginal vision.

Esse in anima is a middle ground partaking of two different aspects—subject/object, inner/outer, observer/observed—but remaining qualitatively separate. From this ground, Jung wrote:

> Living reality is the product neither of the actual, objective behavior of things nor of the formulated idea exclusively, but rather of the combination of both in the living psychological process. (1971, p. 62)

For the Jung of *esse in anima*, the ground of "psychic process," the third world between subject and object, was the image itself (1969a, p. 544). For Jung, meaning lies in the image: "Image represents the *meaning* of the instinct" (1969b, p. 201). "Image and meaning are identical" (ibid., p. 204); image is "a homogenous product with a meaning of its own" (1971, p. 442). From the standpoint of *esse in anima*, Jung finds meaning not in the general and the abstract, but in actual experience in the everyday world as formed through imagination. It is this Jung who said, "[T]he psyche creates reality everyday" (ibid., p. 52).

Ultimately Jung came to see image as the ground of psyche, psyche and image as one, being in image.

> Every psychic process is an image and an "imagining," otherwise no consciousness could exist and the occurrence would lack phenomenality. (1969a, p. 544)

In his last great work, *Mysterium Coniunctionis*, Jung wrote simply, "Images are life" (1963, p. 180). In sum, from the paradigm of *esse in anima*, Jung is saying that all experience occurs through image, through the imagination, and that form and meaning are one.

The postmodern Jung lives and finds meaning through metaphor. We will not see or understand anything until the right metaphor allows it to appear. The term *metaphor* originally signified a concrete activity, that of carrying an object from one place to another. So metaphorical vision always sees an other in what at first appears literal or mundane. We are never just depressed or just frightened; there is always another process going on of which the depression or fear is an expression. It is the metaphorical image that gives meaning and structure to this experience.

In conclusion, when we see through the abstract concepts that Jung used in his rational paradigm—opposition, projection, compensation, typology, masculine/feminine, ego/self, all comforting to subjective consciousness—we see that they too are metaphors, but metaphors without body. In this modernist mode, Jung and Jungians are like midwives responding to a woman in labor with a lecture on the facts of life. The modernist Jung in search of meaning started off with a full-bodied metaphor, the night-sea journey. But it was not until many years later that T. S. Eliot soberly characterized the modern journey as "forever bailing" (from "Dry Salvages," 1952, p. 132) and took the wind out of our sails: "Or say that the end precedes the beginning, / And the end and the beginning were always there / Before the beginning and after the end" (from "Burnt Norton," ibid., p. 121). Likewise, the postmodern Jung saw image, meaning, and being as one.

And so a new image emerges. Now it is no longer the night-sea journey of the hero bringing the light of consciousness. Postmodern consciousness dwells darkly in image—no sooner under way than shipwrecked, now gasping in the night sea, now land-locked in the belly, at once fetus emerging and midwife groping. Jung: "In reality the psyche is the mother and the maker, the subject and even the possibility of consciousness itself" (1969a, p. 84).

Postmodern man, no longer in search, vision coming to rest, dimmed by experience, finds home finally with the ancient Chinese sage Lao-tzu: "Soften the light, become one with the dusty world" (Hillman 1979c, p. 15).

2

THE BODY IN ANALYSIS

BARE BONES—
THE AESTHETICS OF ARTHRITIS

Fleshing Out the Body

Analyzing the body is a strange event. Don't we become embodied only when we play ball or get sick or injured or become adolescent? Most of the time we don't have bodies to analyze; we simply are bodies. We are lived bodies. We live our bodily being, and we are beings living through our bodies. Psyche is body. The body is the happening of our visibility. We can't get away from body to think or talk or write about it. As I write, I am thinking and writing through my body. The body is analytic; the writing is my body arthritic. In attempting to analyze body, depth psychology takes part in a long conceptual tradition that separates body and psyche. This split inevitably forces the body into analysis. It was, after all, the hysterical body that brought the profession of psychotherapy into being. At the same time, the split drives the analytic mind into "body work."

The body-soul split, grounded in a language system that keeps body and soul separate, is not merely as old as Descartes but is as old as the Western tradition itself. Homer uses the word *psyche* to refer to that part of the individual that is active only when the body is dead or inactive. Plato's thought goes through several transformations—soul and body as interaction (*Charmides*), body as "tomb" of the soul (*Gorgias*), and body as "vehicle" of the soul (*Timaeus*). For Aristotle, body is the appearance of soul in matter for the sake of the soul's achievement. The Christian tradition is ambivalent toward the body. On the one hand, it is the temple of the Holy Spirit (I Cor. 6:19), the image of God himself. On the other hand, there is a long tradition linking the body to Satan. In all of these conceptions, body and soul are separate in a hierarchical structure that makes body, at best, serving the ends of soul.

A postmodern arabesque out of the Western tradition is performed by the phenomenologist Maurice Merleau-Ponty, who has attempted the integration of body and soul in concept and language. It is worth taking the time to integrate Merleau-Ponty's meditations on the body into the dialogue of depth psychology. In his early work, Merleau-Ponty (1962, 1963) thought of body and soul as cosignifications, co-relative factors. Body is the mode through which we are present to soul and, at the same time, the means through which soul is present to the world. Body, soul, and world are each indispensable moments of the lived interactional structure that embraces them. Our intentions toward the world find their form in body, while at the same time we perceive in conformity with that very body. As consciousness presents itself through a body, the body becomes the perspectival aspect of being. Body is the mode of actuality of the individual, his or her concrete way of being and manner of inhabiting space and time.

Body is neither pure thing nor pure idea but the "bearer of a dialectic" between the two (Merleau-Ponty 1963, p. 204). Body and soul are not entities but perspectives, contingent upon each other, flowing into and out of each other. But body is also distinct. It becomes distinct when it is "known"—through dysfunction, for example. When body is ill or injured, "the world is doubled," becoming inner and outer (ibid., p. 190). World, body, and perception become distinct entities and then gradually merge back into a unity. El Greco's paintings are not elongated because El Greco was astigmatic, but El Greco's visual disorder was integrated by him into a distinct way of being represented in his paintings.

The body has autonomous being. It

> is and is not ourselves. The body does everything and it does nothing. Neither end nor means. Always involved in matters which go beyond it, always jealous of its autonomy, the body is powerful enough to oppose itself to any merely deliberate end,

yet has none to propose to us if we finally turn toward and con-
sult it. (Merleau-Ponty 1973, p. 112)

As autonomous, body is itself a complex. Body, as a "prepersonal
cleaving to the general form of the world, as an anonymous and
general existence, plays, beneath my personal life, the part of an
inborn complex" (Merleau-Ponty 1962, p. 84).

    As complex, body is a unique structure of experience, the
experience of material being, bearing history. The pastness of experience is carried into the present through the body, or, through
the body, the present remains in the past. The ambiguity of being
in the world in both the past and present simultaneously is taken
up by the body.

> It can now be said that, *a fortiori*, the specific past, which our
> body is, can be recaptured and taken up by an individual life only
> because that life has never transcended it, but secretly nourishes
> it, devoting thereto part of its strength, because its present is still
> that past. (Merleau-Ponty 1962, p. 85)

The body is the "third term" in the figure-background structure between consciousness and world (ibid., p. 101). It is the ground for
experience, the darkness upon which experience is inscribed, the
flesh of the world that inscribes upon the world. Body is what
makes space, what makes world. It is our opening onto the world,
our "rising toward the world" (ibid., p. 92), the "collecting together
of itself in pursuit of its aims" (ibid., p. 101).

    Existence realizes itself in the body. It is not that my red
face or clenched fist signify anger. The face and the fist are the
anger. The meaning is not behind the appearance or gesture, but is
"intermingled with the structure of the world outlined by the gesture" (Merleau-Ponty 1962, p. 186). Neither the body nor consciousness can be considered originative or causative since they
presuppose each other to begin with. Body is existence solidified,
and existence is a perpetual incarnation. Body is the "woven fabric"
of existence, the "mirror of being" (ibid., pp. 166, 171). It is the
unique manner in which I relate to the world and through which
my experience is shaped and styled, while at the same time the
world is encrusted in the body.

> The experience of our own body . . . reveals to us an ambiguous
> mode of existing . . . I have no means of knowing the human
> body other than that of living it, which means taking up on my
> own account the drama which is being played out of it, and los-
> ing myself in it. I am my body at least wholly to the extent that I
> possess experience, and yet at the same time my body is as it
> were a "natural" subject, a provisional sketch of my total being.
> (Ibid., p. 198)

Here Merleau-Ponty's "body" mirrors certain aspects of
Jung's "body." Jung said, "The body is a visible expression of the
here and now" (Jung 1976, p. 475) and "the body is merely the visibility of the soul, the psyche, and the soul is the psychological experience of the body; so it is really one and the same thing" (Jung,
quoted by Jarrett 1981, pp. 199–200). As paradoxically lived and
known, "autonomous," "complex," "drama," Merleau-Ponty's body
reflects Jung's notions of psyche, giving us a clue to the psychological being of body, body as the unconscious itself, or body as the
depth in the surface.

In Merleau-Ponty's later work, body is no longer an interactional element with soul or the medium of the dialectic between
experience and world; it is at once the "intertwining" or the "chiasm" between the two. It is neither matter nor signifier of psyche,
but the visible and the invisible at once.

> We mean that carnal being, as a being of depths, of several leaves
> or several faces, a being in latency, and a presentation of a certain
> absence, is a prototype of Being, of which our body, the sensible
> sentient, is a very remarkable variant, but whose constitutive para-
> dox already lies in every visible. (Merleau-Ponty 1968, p. 136)

Body as a "prototype of Being" would parallel body as a prototype
of the self in Jungian terms. For Merleau-Ponty, body has now become "flesh," not corpuscles nor psychic material brought into
being, but the reciprocity between the seer and the seen, so that
one no longer knows which is which.

> To designate it, we should need the old term, "element," in the
> sense it was used to speak of water, air, earth, and fire, that is, in
> the sense of a *general thing*, midway between the spatio-temporal
> individual and the idea, a sort of incarnate principle that brings a

style of being wherever there is a fragment of being. (Merleau-Ponty 1968, p. 139)

Flesh is the prototype of Being that circles between visibility and invisibility. It is the "bond between the visible and the interior armature which it manifests and which it conceals" (ibid., p. 149), the lining and the depth of the invisible.

The thickness of body is the opening into the world. It is not so much that which perceives, but that which is "built around the perception that dawns through it," the "cohesion of depth of the world" (Merleau-Ponty 1968, pp. 9, 112). As entrance into the world, it is not so much adherent to the here and now, but the "inauguration of where and when, the possibility and exigency of fact" or the "occasion" of ideas (ibid., pp. 150–1). "It is the invisible of the world, that which inhabits this world, sustains it and renders it visible, its own and interior possibility, the Being of this being" (ibid.).

In summary, through Merleau-Ponty's meditations on body, we have moved from a notion of body as an integral part of body-soul dialectic to body as a third realm, a mode of vision, a style of being. Merleau-Ponty has helped us to fashion a way of seeing body, namely, body as a way of seeing, through which we can now envision one particular mode of being, that of arthritis.

The Arthritic Aesthetic

I am

tracked,

laser resolute,

duty-bound, mummified in

responsibility. Upholding

obligation, committed

like a titan

supporting.

When the heavens lie within,

where can Psyche show,

how display?

She comes slowly,

subtly,

relentless

grinding cushy links

that wear away

like the tread of a tire travelled too far.

As bone sculpture

Psyche presents

forged,

fire in the water

gargoyle

emerging core

cries

"No more, no more."

—an arthritic patient

Etymologically, "arthritis" comes from the Greek, meaning inflammation of the *arthron* or joint. The word first appears in medieval times to designate pain caused by a faulty flow of the humors. "Rheumatic" means to suffer from a flux, a flow, a rheum, or fluid. The Greek word *rheumatismos* designates an evil humor or mucous that was thought to flow from the brain to the joint. Galen used the term "rheumatic" to designate pain caused by one of the four humors in faulty connection with the others or flowing from the brain into the blood and being discharged into the cavities of the body.

Arthritis is an autoimmune disease, the body becoming allergic to itself. It begins insidiously and progresses slowly, bringing about a relentless metamorphosis of the body into a skewed and rigid form. Lymphocytes from the bloodstream begin to attack not only antigens or foreign substances but also the structural tissue around the joint. Another group of blood cells, macrophages, are called to the scene in increasing numbers. These cells secrete enzymes that eat away at cartilage. The joint becomes a scene of war, the body attacking itself, expressing its conflict in stiffness, pain, tenderness of the joint, cloudy fluid in the joint lining, swelling, nodules under the skin, which takes on a cold, clammy feel. Inflammation and liquidation, fire and water, appear as one. The patient has a mild fever and a vague feeling of malaise. As the cartilage or intermediary tissue is eaten away, bone ends grind

against each other, eventually fusing. Muscles atrophy, the joint becomes useless, and grotesque deformities of bone appear.

The etiology of arthritis is unknown. It is not communi-
cable, no particular blood factor can be found, nor has it been
linked to genetic origins. Medically oriented psychologists have hy-
pothesized neurological dysfunction as a source of two symptoms
found in arthritic patients: the inability to express feelings and the
inability to fantasize (Achterberg and Lawlis 1980, pp. 266–273). To
be unable to express feelings is referred to medically as *alexithymia*, meaning "without words for feelings." From the medical or
causal view, this condition is due to a structural defect rather than
to self-imposed restraint or unconscious repression of feeling, the
structural defect being seen as a lesion in the prefrontal lobe or
frontolimbic pathways. The neural pathways of the soma would
thus respond exclusively, without evoking a response in the corti-
cal areas that interpret sensory events. In other words, a short cir-
cuit from lower to higher pathways is suggested, feelings
transcribed directly into physical symptoms rather than words.

Arthritis is also linked to an inability to fantasize, the term
for which is *pense operatoire*. This condition is exemplified in the
relatively meager drawings that arthritic patients make of their disease. Again, the causal view of this condition would look for a
structural defect or learning disability as the source.

Perhaps as much as any disease of the soma, arthritis has
also been linked causally with factors of the psyche. Two of the
early explorers in psychosomatic medicine worked in the field of
arthritis. Stanley Jeliffe, an Austrian psychoanalyst, analyzed an
arthritic patient in the 1920s. He took before-and-after x-rays of the
bone structure of his patient's leg to prove the efficacy of psychoanalysis. Richard Halliday was a British medical insurance investi-
gator in the 1930s and 1940s who was among the first to come up
with a cohesive personality profile of the arthritic patient. Among
his findings was the fact that, in Scotland, people of the Calvinist
faith were much more likely to develop arthritis than the popula-
tion at large.

Medical literature over the past few decades abounds in
various descriptions of the arthritic personality profile, but there is
much controversy over methodology. Central to the arthritic mode
seems to be an inherent conflict between flexibility and rigidity.

The individual is tirelessly active, seeming to work day and night, on the job and at home, in self-sacrificing service to others. At the same time, the personality of the arthritic has been described as emotionally restricted, calm, quiet, and excessively patient. He or she has difficulty verbalizing feelings of anger and often seems emotionally restricted or indifferent to his or her situation.

The background of the arthritic patient typically includes an early life characterized by an excessive amount of physical activity and/or athletics. The patient has an affinity for orderliness, punctuality, and tidiness. His or her past characteristically includes a strict and uncompromising mother and a weak or absent father. There is evidence of an inadequate sense of individual identity, and severe emotional deprivation in early life. The patient is said to have strong dependency needs that are kept hidden behind a rigid facade of character armor that proclaims autonomy and independence.

An aesthetic view of arthritis would see through a causal notion of the disease, whether the source be somatic or psychic, to its mythical and classical background. The figures and motifs found in myth and history give body to the disease and validate it as, in itself, a form or way of life. The fiery attack of the lymphocytes on the joint lining speaks of heroic activism gone berserk, Hercules madly slaying even his own kind. The rigid upholding of obligation bespeaks Atlas, whose name is derived from the word meaning "to bear." (The word for the cells that eat away at the cartilage, macrophage, literally means "giant eater.") The interplay between the dynamic and the rigid in the arthritic state, then, can be seen as an interplay between the Herculean mode on the one hand and Atlas on the other—dynamic and static.

As the chronic disease par excellence, the disease of middle and old age, proceeding on a slow, relentless, linear course toward making the body concrete, arthritis can be seen primarily as a revealing of the old king, Kronos. His is an image of exile and fixedness. His temperament is cold, reflected in a distant affect as well as in the clammy skin of the arthritic. Cold is harsh reality—no fantasy here, just things as they are, literally, positively, and materialistically. Kronos's concern is for structure, upholding tradition and order. The rigidity of Kronos is not just the stiff upper lip and stiff-jointedness of the arthritic but also the ego-certainty of "I know" reflected in the arthritic's invulnerability to change. The perpetual suffering of Kronos is reflected in the "chronic" pain of the arthritic.

Immediately adjacent to the configuration of Kronos in the archetypal background of arthritic consciousness as a way of life is the philosophical doctrine of Stoicism (Ziegler 1983). Stoicism existed as an active school of philosophy from the beginning of the Hellenistic Age, 300 B.C., to the decline of the Roman Empire in 300 A.D. As the arch-philosophy of the spirit, it was the chief rival of Epicureanism, the arch-philosophy of the material. The main precept of the Stoic view was "life according to nature" or life in accordance with cold reality, we might say. The Stoic strove to attain autocracy or self-sufficiency in the face of the world and identified with the divine. The body was considered an encumbrance to divine reason, and the Stoic strove to treat it with indifference. Stoic apathy is an imperviousness to perturbations from both the concrete, outer world and the inner world of emotion and fantasy. A person must pay attention only to what is within his or her power, namely will.

In the lives and writings of Zeno of Citium, Epictetus, and Marcus Aurelius, we can see the Stoic aesthetic as a background for the psychology of arthritis. Zeno was known for his great powers of abstinence and endurance. His habits were simple; he lived on uncooked food and wore a thin cloak no matter what the weather. A poem about him reads:

> The cold of winter and the ceaseless rain,
> Come powerless against him; weak is the dart
> Of the fierce summer sun, or fell disease,
> To bend that iron frame. He stands apart,
> In nought resembling the vast common crowd,
> But patient and unwearied, night and day,
> Clings to his studies and philosophy.

> (Hadas 1961, p. 11)

This description serves as a motto for the Stoic and the arthritic, pledging obedience to interior virtue. The rigidity and hardness of this personality reflect the rigid structuralization of the arthritic body.

Epictetus was a slave who spread his message by evangelizing to crowds. His manual was transcribed from his oratory by one of his disciples. Among his sayings are the following:

> Disease is an impediment to the body, but not to the will, unless the will itself chooses. Lameness is an impediment to the leg, but not to the will. (Hadas 1961, p. 87)

> Remember that in life you ought to behave as at a banquet. Suppose that something is carried round and is opposite to you. Stretch out your hand and take a portion with decency. Suppose that it passes by you. Do not detain it. Suppose that it is not yet come to you. Do not send your desire forward to it, but wait till it is opposite you. (Ibid., p. 88)

For Epictetus, an individual has no say in the course of his or her life. Ever self-effacing, the Stoic plays the role chosen by another. Emotion, body, and world are all to be fought against. The philosopher "watches himself as if he were an enemy" (ibid., p. 99). It is as if those heroic warrior lymphocytes of the arthritic body were under the direct command of Epictetus as they attack the joint lining.

In contrast to Epictetus, the slave who spoke to throngs, Marcus Aurelius was an emperor who wrote only for himself. In his diary he advocated abstinence from pleasure and desire and emphasized the transitory quality of life and the bounds of nature. His image of the ideal person is like the rigidly protruding arthritic bone: "Be like the promontory against which the waves continually break, but it stands firm and tames the fury of the water around it" (Hadas 1961, p. 131). Or, in more detail,

> Are you angry with him whose armpits stink? Are you angry with him whose mouth smells foul? What good will this anger do you? He has such a mouth, he has such armpits: it is necessary that such an emanation must come from such things. (Ibid., p. 139)

We speak of the arthritic's inability to fantasize as a symptom, but Aurelius says, "Wipe out the imagination. Stop the pulling of the strings. Confine yourself to the present" (ibid., p. 155).

In summary, in the same way that the notion of an "arthritic personality" takes us away from a strictly biological view of symptomatology, the aesthetic view that sees the mythic and Stoic perspective in the background of arthritis moves us away from the notion of arthritis as merely pathology or compensation. Instead, arthritis becomes the presentation of the body itself, soul bodying forth and reflecting a way of being.

To see the aesthetics of arthritis requires what Baudelaire called the "intimate eye." The intimate eye is the eye of sculptor Henry Moore, who speaks of the importance of the emotion inherent in the form of an art object rather than in its representational value. It is the eye of the impressionist painter Pierre Bonnard, who said that the subject of a painting is its surface, with colors and laws over and above those of the object. The intimate eye would see the arthritic body much as T. S. Eliot describes "the weakness of the changing body" as "the (woven) enchainment of past and future" ("Burnt Norton," 1952). With the intimate eye, ornamentation would not be seen as the adornment of joints with bracelets, wristbands, and neckwear, symbolically representative of the relationship between articulation and rigidity. Rather, the bones themselves would be seen as adornment, Psyche's display of herself for the beholding eye.

If sculpture is the arthritic medium that most purely combines dynamics and structure, then the arthritic form becomes the blending of the dynamics of heroism with the titanic upholding of structure. The arthritic body becomes both the sculpture and the artist. *Pense operatoire* would be seen not with a bias toward the rich, vivid, burgeoning imagination that one finds in cancer patients. Rather, it would be seen with an appreciation for the barebones imagination, the imagination of no imagination. Rather than seeing alexithymia through a tradition of talking as cure, the aesthetic eye would perceive silence itself as a mode of being. The silence of the arthritic would bespeak a level of experience at which words fail. Through the tight jaw and the stiff upper lip, the arthritic would be telling us of that which is unutterable in our day-to-day existence, unutterably private, unutterably unique, unutterably horrific. Here, the showing forth of bones becomes that which is art itself, the necessarily inarticulate cry. Here, aesthetics becomes something not separate from, nor tangential to, understanding, but that which is the meaning itself.

To appreciate the arthritic aesthetic, we would need to start from a place where the perception of image is a primary mode of eros or empathy or healing. We would need to see the pain of the arthritic as a style of suffering inherent in a particular mode of being and honor the potential in that pain, just as we honor the potential in the form of modern sculpture. It is an approach that is neither cruel nor kind, one that seeks connection not in feeling but in seeing. Our starting point, like that of the Greeks, is not the separation of the good from the beautiful, or the beautiful from the useful, but in the vision of them as one and the same. We would need to leave aside notions of beauty as harmony, balance, or symmetry and adjust our gaze to see the perfection inherent in the individual form. Like Rilke, we would see that "Beauty is nothing / but the beginning of Terror which we are still just able to bear" ("The First Elegy," 1939). We would come to an appreciation of the aesthetic particular to the grotesque—the gnarled, knotted forms of the grotto, cave, or underworld. These forms can be appreciated for themselves, not by an eye that penetrates, seeking meaning in an ultimate source, an eye anchored in a system of transcendent wholeness, but by the eye adrift, sensuous in its touch, the eye of the eroticized mind.

The Voluptuous Gaze

The following passage occurs in Yukio Mishima's autobiographical novel, *Sun and Steel*.

> Why should the area of the skin, which guarantees a human being's existence in space, be most despised and left to the tender mercies of the senses? I could not understand the law governing the motion of thought—the way it was liable to get stuck in unseen chasms whenever it set out to go deep; or whenever it aimed at the heights, to soar away into boundless and equally invisible heavens, leaving the corporeal form undeservedly neglected.
>
> If the law of thought is that it should search out profundity, whether it extends upwards or downwards, then it seemed excessively illogical to me that men should not discover depths of a kind on the "surface," that vital borderline that endorses our separateness and our form, dividing our exterior from our interior. Why should they not be attracted by the profundity of the surface itself? (1970, pp. 22–23)

Something there is in the Western mind that distrusts surface. Platonic vision places essence beyond appearance and moves from appearance itself to universals beyond. Gnosticism calls for the release of soul from within the prison of the body to the heavens above. Christianity declares the kingdom of Heaven to be within. Technological investigation looks for causes in inner workings. Modern medicine probes into the body as does psychoanalysis into the psyche. (Both Freud and Jung likened the analyst to the surgeon.) Our language system, through which our very being is formed, is based on the metaphysical movement from word to meaning. The quest for the source—above, below, behind, and beyond—works to prevent recognition of what is most obvious, appearance. The vision of quest serves to hinder the revelation that occurs in the immediate presentation of things as they are.

The field of biology and the work of the Swiss biologist Adolf Portmann take us further in thinking about an aesthetic mode of perceiving and relating it to the body. Portmann's observations of plants and animals have led him to postulate an innate urge toward self-expression in nature. In the multitude of outer appearances of animals and plants, he sees not primarily a species-preserving function but a display of form. The living form of the animal, which not only maintains its life and propagates its kind, but also presents its special manner of existence, its world.

The philosopher Alphonso Lingis delineates "world":

A world, a cosmos, is the order, the ordinance extending according to axes of close and far, intimate and alien, upwards and downwards, lofty and base, right and left, auspicious and inauspicious, within which things can have their places, show their aspects and stake out paths. (1983, p. 3)

For Portmann, the most modest plant expresses its independent being, its world, in the shape and coloration of its leaf, flower, and fruit. Tiny aquatic organisms express their essences in a host of splendid forms and colors. The simplest of mollusks manifests itself in the most splendid and ornate of shells. Portmann asserts that this urge toward display in nature operates independently of anything related to functionality. The survival of species cannot explain the ornate coils of an elaborate rack of antlers. The splendid feather patterns of the peacock do not play an important part in mating but seem to be part of an exhibitionistic scheme that exists for its own sake.

In sum, Portmann takes seriously the fact that prior to all utilitarian conceptions of the preservation of species, what we encounter first and foremost is the straightforward appearance of the living being in its full form, what Lingis calls the "logic of ostentation" (1983, p. 8). Nature serves the beholding eye of the other. Lingis writes:

> Glory is for its witness, the spectacle is for the spectator, the screen of phenomenal effects produced in reality are for a sphere of lucidity, an eye, a mind! With this inference one makes even the gloss of appearance intelligible, and one posits oneself as an essential and necessary factor in the sphere which one enters. One appropriates even this film of semblance and this vanity of appearances. *Omnia ad amiorem gloriam deo*—God himself was said to have been obliged to create man to receive the splendor of his glory. (Ibid., p. 9)

Freud saw libido's original manifestation as being a matter of *surface* excitement, the pleasure of the polymorphously perverse infant in couplings for the sake of tactile effects, a horizontal movement from one contact point to another. In its earliest condition, eros seeks form in appearance.

The aesthetic view would not look to the surface for its symbolic content, deflecting one's view off into the depths, on toward the horizon, out toward the universal where their signified referents, sources, and meanings are posited to be. Instead it is a gaze that caresses and is caressed in reciprocity with the world. It is the gaze of the sensualized mind, in foreplay with the surface.

In order to give us a glimpse of what the eroticized universe is like, Lingis takes us to the ancient Hindu temples of Khajuraho in India. Here one finds wall upon wall of friezes depicting a universe of possibilities of *coniunctio*: "dual and multiple cunnilinctio, penilinctio, copulation, homosexual and bestial intercourse circulate about the temple walls without primacy of place or of artistry given to any one figure" (Lingis 1983, p. 59). Here the 8,400,000 forms of animal positions that are the foundation for the 8,400,000 asanas of Patanjali's classical hatha yoga are all taken as human possibilities. Here the human body not only makes contact with every other organic form, but each separate and unique form of the individual body has relationship with each unique form of every other body. "The human form here is not treated as a single design whose spatial configuration expresses statically a dynamical axis or nexus of force" (ibid., p. 63). Rather, each peculiar form is portrayed in its own perfection. The dissymmetry of sexes shown in the friezes is not a practice of power or ascendance, as men bearing vulvas and women with penile erections alternate and reciprocate in initiation and reception. One makes love with animals, without descending, and with the gods, without ascending. The gaze does not travel up or down, penetrate or detach; it circulates aimlessly, drifting, holding the reverberations between forms.

What is revealed at Khajuraho through the depiction of human bodies in supple, erotic connection with the universe is a bodily way of seeing, being as seeing, seeing as embodied, seeing/being/body—all one. The question then becomes not one of the "body in analysis," but how does analysis become embodied? Seeing erotically undermines the priority we give to the question "What to do?" because this vision sees all doing as inherently seeing. We do as we see. Seeing here is not passive observation and acceptance, any more than the vision of the artist is passive. The therapist sees what presents itself—in the psychological life of the patient, in the reverberations of the therapist's own psyche, or in the imaginative realm of the interaction between therapist and patient. The work is not so much an application of technique as a deconstruction of what gets in the way of seeing.

The interpretive mode and "body work" go hand in hand, manifesting and perpetuating the central split of our cultural heritage—body and soul, surface and depth, inner and outer, sacred and profane. It is the consciousness that separates aesthetics from epistemology, art from understanding, what I do from how I see. To speak of links between the unconscious and the body between imaginative consciousness and bodily perception, or of "subtle body" or "imaginative body" only maintains the split, serving the fallen vision of Satan in William Blake's sense.

The medium is the massage, and the rub is in the gaze. The "body in analysis" is no different from the body anywhere else. All

perception, all imagination is bodily perception, bodily imagination, while at the same time the body is the imagination, is the
view.

"Body?"

"No need to worry. It's there—in the gap . . . in the chiasm
. . . in the intertwining. Now visible, now invisible. Here."

"Where?"

"Here, in the vision, floating in 'happy copulation' (from
"Visions of the Daughters of Albion," Blake 1965, p. 49), seeing a
world in a single bare bone."

"Body? There. Where?"

"Play ball"—

3

A GROUND FOR PSYCHE

Phenomenology is a postmodern philosophy that emerged during the first half of the twentieth century with the work of its founding fathers, Edmund Husserl, Martin Heidegger, and Maurice Merleau-Ponty. This chapter will further elaborate the glimpse we had in chapter 1 into Jung's phenomenological orientation. Contemporaneous not only in time but in historical necessity with Jung's thought, phenomenology emerged in response to the materialism, positivism, and Cartesian rationalism of the modern mind. The foundation of phenomenology, simply stated, is a vision that is as free as possible from underlying preconceptions, governing concepts or constructs, and dogmatic theory. The approach of phenomenology is to understand an individual phenomenon from the standpoint of the ontological ground from which it appears, its mode of being in the world, using the method of knowing that takes direct description as its starting point.

In 1970, Paul Ricoeur, phenomenologist and linguist, published a classic series of lectures using Freud's ideas to explore language—specifically hermeneutic language. In that exploration, Ricoeur found that psychoanalytic language, embodying a "hermeneutics of suspicion" when regarding Cartesian consciousness in its immediacy, seemed to be in opposition to phenomenology, which started with a "hermeneutics of belief." In other words, whereas psychoanalysis seems to approach meaning through a perceived gap between what is consciously reported and what is unconsciously revealed, phenomenology starts with faith in conscious experience.

On closer examination, however, Ricoeur concluded that

phenomenology and psychoanalysis are more often alike in their in-
direct approach to naive consciousness. First, because it suspends
conceptual ground in the service of an understanding governed by
the event or thing itself, phenomenology, like psychoanalysis, manages to provide a "humiliation or wounding" of immediate consciousness. The purpose of this wounding is to reveal the concealed
or "co-intended" aspect of consciousness, what psychoanalysis might
see as unconscious motivation (Ricoeur 1970, pp. 377–8). Second,
both phenomenology and psychoanalysis hold to a notion of intentionality, namely, the "intending" of consciousness for an "other" outside of itself. The psychoanalytic view sees the unconscious intent as
desire *for* an object; the phenomenological view sees consciousness
as awareness *of* something. In other words, in phenomenology there
is no consciousness per se; rather, subjectivity and object of consciousness are always linked. Third, both phenomenology and psychoanalysis find an ambivalent reality unfolding in language as a
dialectic of presence and absence (ibid., p. 384). Words are absent as
signs or signifiers of meaning and present as living symbols that form
a concealed or unconscious world. Finally, both phenomenology
and psychoanalysis hold to a sense of the intersubjectivity of meaning, namely, meaning is such only "insofar as the implicit is what another can make explicit" (ibid., p. 386). Indeed, for Ricoeur, the goal
of both psychoanalysis and phenomenology is "the return to true discourse" (ibid., quoting De Waelhens, p. 390). In summary, Ricoeur's
achievement was to see psychoanalysis and phenomenology each
through the eyes of the other.

Ricoeur opened Freud's work to phenomenological analysis
by seeing in it the dialectic of two languages—the language of science (biological foundations, dynamics of forces) and the language
of meaning (hermeneutic constructs such as id, ego, superego). As
we saw in chapter 1, two views of psychological reality—rationality
and meaning—are also revealed in the work of the other great
founder of depth psychology, C. G. Jung. The first is a conceptual
universe—a quasi-scientific world that, in the service of empiricism,
splits observer from observed, reasserts a formal theory expound-
ing mechanistic structures and the dynamics of energies based on
nineteenth-century physics, proposes psychic systems of oppositions and logocentrism based on the metaphysics of the classical
concept of proportion, and provides abstract, often tautological,

Aristotelian categories of definition. Jung's second ontology is a poetic realm that he termed "*esse in anima*," a middle ground encompassing both subject and object which declares the reality of fantasy, metaphor, and imagination.

The mixture of these two ontologies in Jung's work has caused some confusion in the Jungian world (Samuels 1985). Following in the Cartesian heritage of modern Western thought, classical Jungians have taken Jung's conceptualizations as though they were meant to be literal, and they have built modular paradigms around the definition and redefinition of Jung's conceptual assertions. Archetypal psychology, founded with the work of James Hillman, emerged in reaction to this approach (Hillman 1977, 1978, 1979a, 1979b, 1980). By making ontological distinctions in Jung's work, Hillman has been able to demonstrate how Jung's grounding in imagination gives a psychological view of experience, while his leanings toward conceptualization tends, rather dangerously, to empower and enhance the observing ego in a nonpsychological way.

Roger Brooke (1991) continues in the tradition of Ricoeur and Hillman by attempting to see through Jung's work, this time with the eye of phenomenology. Brooke's assertion is that Jung, in attempting to stake out ground for psychological reality, was forced by the limitations of his conceptual background and by his need to gain general recognition for his ideas to use the very language of conceptual logic that he was intuitively trying to undermine. By deriving meaning through the application of concepts, or, in the alchemical sense, by extracting spirit from matter, Jung's writing often depicts human beings as though they were material bodies separate from an outer world, encapsulated entities containing energies and forces working mysteriously within. In this depiction, psyche becomes trapped in body and separated from a world that is dead, and care of the soul through analysis becomes the application of a grid of concepts onto disembodied experience. In this mode, Jungian psychology "tends to perpetuate in its conceptual foundations an image of Cartesian man: an isolate in his experience standing over a meaningless, homogenous world" (Brooke 1991, p. 114).

Seeing Jung's work through the lens of phenomenology allows something different to emerge—an image of Jung as psychological poet, setting forth experience itself as meaningful and finding the expression of experience through metaphor as the basic data of psychological life. Even as Jung was explaining himself in logical constructs, something in his work was striving for articulation through phenomenological expression—the meaning inherent in the "pregnant immediacy" of the phenomenon itself (Brooke 1991, p. 7). In the phenomenological paradigm, inner and outer become a unity, which phenomenology calls the "life world," and the psyche becomes the ground for all experience working through human consciousness in metaphors. (Of course, this sounds very much like archetypal psychology, and one of Brooke's insights is to see Hillman, who emphasizes "saving the phenomena," as a healer of Jung's thought.) Seen phenomenologically, Jung becomes a poet of the soul, a craftsman working in the mode of imagination with an "intrinsic, irreducible, and mutually transformative relationship between him and his subject matter" (ibid.).

Because Jung actually stands with a foot in each paradigm, a tension emerges between the way he talks about meaning and the way he talks about experience. Jung's quasi-scientific mode conflicts with his poorly expressed, imaginal, relativistic sense of the coparticipation of observer-observed. (This latter epistemology, which derives from mediumistic psychology, is never clearly worked out in Jung, who sometimes even denigrates it as *participation mystique*.) The poetry of the latter mode needs conceptual tightening, and it is this tightening that Brooke sees as the gift of phenomenology—a contribution that grants the poetic side of Jung's thought both an epistemological (metaphor) and ontological (life-world) foundation.

Maurice Merleau-Ponty's classic definition of phenomenology, contained in the preface to his book, *The Phenomenology of Perception* (1962), portrays it as a method for studying the essences of phenomena based on four characteristics: description, reduction, search for essence, and intentionality. Each of these characteristics can be related to Jung's method. Phenomenology is basically a descriptive enterprise, "obsessed by the concrete" (Brooke 1991, quoting Van den Berg, p. 31), and as such is distrustful of all theoretical assumptions and conceptual orientations. Description in phenomenology is not a naive, positivistic categorization of observables, but the disciplined return of a "second naivete" to the phenomenon itself so that it may reveal itself in ever deeper, richer, more subtle and more complex ways (Ricoeur 1970, p. 28). In this light, Jung discloses himself as a phenomenologist in his forceful exposition of religious experience as fact (1969a, pp. 5–7) and in his criticism of Freud's way of placing theory over experience (1968a, pp. 54–55). Nowhere is Jung's allegiance to actual experience clearer than in his famous statement regarding the dream: "Stick as close as possible to the dream image" (1966a, p. 149).

A more formal characteristic of phenomenology is the step in thought that Husserl called "the phenomenological reduction," which involves two aspects, the "bracketing of being" (or the "epoché") and the return to "original experience." "Bracketing," for Husserl, is a separation from the "natural attitude" in which prejudices and preconceptions that are concealed hinder access to an understanding of phenomena as they present themselves to naive consciousness. The return to "our most original experience of our most original world" (Brooke 1991, quoting Luijpen, p. 33) is like Hillman's "animal perception," the direct experience of the world unencumbered by concepts (Hillman 1979a).

Jung's sensibility to what phenomenology refers to as "reduction" can be seen throughout his career, and Brooke provides ample documentation, such as Jung's advice in 1912 to the budding psychologist to

> abandon exact science, put away his scholar's gown, bid farewell to his study, and wander with human heart through the world. There, in the horrors of prisons, lunatic asylums and hospitals, in drab suburban pubs, in brothels and gambling halls, in the salons of the elegant, the Stock Exchanges, Socialist meetings, churches revivalist gatherings and ecstatic sects, through love and hate, through the experience of passion in every form in his own body, he would reap richer stores of knowledge than text-books a foot thick could give him, and he will know how to doctor the sick with real knowledge of the human soul. (Jung 1966b, pp. 246–247)

Forty-five years later Jung expresses a similar approach to the analytic situation.

> If I want to understand an individual human being, I must lay aside all scientific knowledge of the average man and discard all theories in order to adopt a completely new and unprejudiced

attitude. I can only approach the task of understanding with a free
and open mind. (Jung 1964, p. 250)

More succinctly Jung said, "nothing is more unbearable to the patient than to be always understood . . . . Understanding should
. . . be . . . an agreement which is the fruit of joint reflection"
(1966a, pp. 145–146).

   Both phenomenology and Jung are aware of the limits imposed by the human condition on achieving the phenomenological
reduction. Jung often pointed out the paradox that since only the
psyche can ask questions regarding the psyche, what psyche shows
of itself is always in a sense a reflection of the psyche that is asking
the question. "[O]ne is oneself the biggest of all one's assumptions"
(Jung 1966a, p. 329). Jung considered complexes, which inevitably
influence one's perceptions, as "the most absolutely prejudiced
thing in every individual" (Jung 1969b, p. 103).

   A third characteristic of phenomenological investigation,
often more difficult to conceptualize, is Husserl's "eidetic reduction," which Brooke helpfully terms "the search for essence" (in itself a Jungian idea). This is the process wherein the essence of a
thing or event is revealed through a meditative, intuitive, imaginative perception. Ricoeur points out that the notion of a concealed
essence is very much akin to what depth psychology considers "the
unconscious" and that the eidetic reduction is akin to analysis. Phenomenology, however, considers essences to be given with the
phenomena themselves, depth lying in the surface. Essence is intuited by a naive consciousness, revealed through the mode of imagination and made up of meaningful relations. Intuition, of course, is
not pure perception but, like all perception, an interpretation
which in itself is co-constituted by language. Thus, for phenomenology, the world is not a dead object described through the lifeless tool of language but a living event simultaneously revealed/
manifested/perceived/interpreted through metaphor.

   Jung's kinship with the phenomenologist's "search for
essence" lies in his hermeneutical approach to the psyche. As a
phenomenologist, Jung was interested in understanding the psyche
on its own terms. He considered pathological behavior, bodily
symptoms, love affairs, the therapeutic relationship, and dreams as
texts to be understood, and he saw that the language that best pro-

vides a link with the vital roots of psychological experience was psyche's own traditional language—religious symbol, myth, fairy tale, and alchemical image. Like the phenomenologist, Jung stepped back from the concretistic standpoint by cautioning against confusing the metaphorical nature of experience with the literal: "every interpretation necessarily remains an 'as-if'" (Jung 1968a, p. 156). Likewise, Jung intuited the constitutive force of language itself: "[i]nterpretations make use of certain linguistic matrices that are themselves derived from primordial images" (ibid., pp. 32–33).[1]

A final aspect of the phenomenological method is derived from the idea of intentionality—all consciousness is a consciousness *of* something. In other words, there is no split between "consciousness" and "something" to begin with; each co-constitutes the event.

> In short, consciousness is that irreducible, non-optional occurrence within which the world comes into being. It cannot be an encapsulated entity, enclosed within itself, or a little person looking at images in the brain. As being-in-the-world, consciousness is the open clearing that gathers the world together. Its constitutive power is that such a world is gathered together in history, culture, and language, as well as through the peculiar twists of individual lives, and it is out of that gathered world-disclosure that we come to understand ourselves as the persons we are. (Brooke 1991, p. 43)

Accepting this constitutive role of consciousness affects how we analyze consciousness and the importance we assign to it. Jung had an intuitive grasp of the unity of psyche and world and saw several important consequences for psychological analysis. First, the withdrawal of projection becomes not so much a mechanical extraction of life from world to psyche but a shift in *mode* of experiencing from literal to metaphorical. Second, although he often seems to be imagining psyche as within, Jung also writes in a way that indicates we are *in* psyche. Third, Jung's focus on the separation of the ego from the unconscious is finally in the aim of revealing of world, that is, the unique place of the human ego in the scheme of things comes about *simultaneously* with the emergence of world.

Interestingly in light of Hillman's (1980) criticism of typology, Brooke sees Jung's notion of typology as a further indication of his intellectual kinship with the phenomenological notion of intentionality. In Jung's model of consciousness there is no perception of the world that is not typologically limited, and this suggests a structural unity encompassing consciousness and world. Typology can be seen as "a measure of shifting values and intensities in one's relation to the world" (Brooke 1991, p. 44). Jung wrote directly to the issue.

> The book on types yielded the insight that every judgement made by an individual is conditioned by his personality type and that every point of view is necessarily relative. (1961, p. 207)

Jung's sensibility to relativity is highlighted in his notion of fantasy as the

> medium that integrates one's psychological functions and brings both the constitutive power of one's psychological life and the world into being . . . . [F]antasy in analytical psychology is the definitive quality of that "between" out of which the world and one's sense of oneself (ego) emerge and are derived. (Brooke 1991, pp. 46–47)

For both Jung and phenomenology, experience and understanding come together in fantasy.[2] It is appropriate here to address the subject in more detail since it is the foundation of the alternative that phenomenology and depth psychology present to scientific reason. Heidegger indicates the *co-constitution* of experience and understanding at their primary levels.

> State-of-mind is *one* of the existential structures in which the Being of the "there" maintains itself. Equiprimordial with it in constituting this Being is *understanding*. A state-of-mind always has its understanding, even if it merely keeps it suppressed. Understanding always has its mood. (Heidegger 1962, p. 182)

The disclosing or revealing (*aletheia*) of a world in any one instant of consciousness is already an understanding of that world.

Jung's contribution to the phenomenological claim that all perception is a kind of understanding is to have seen understanding as a mode of fantasy. "The psyche creates reality every day. The only expression I can use for this activity is *fantasy*" (Jung

1971, p. 52). Further, as we saw in chapter 1, Jung designates experience as a matter of "imaging" and image as the carrier of its own meaning.

> Every psychic process is an image and an imaging, otherwise no consciousness could exist and the concurrence would lack phenomenality. (Jung 1969a, p. 544)

> Image represents the meaning of instinct. (Jung 1969b, p. 204)

> Image and meaning are identical, and as the first takes shape, the latter becomes clear. (Ibid., p. 201)

> (Image is) a homogenous product with a meaning of its own. (Jung 1971, p. 442)

The result is that we are "so wrapped about by psychic images that . . . all knowledge consists of the stuff of the psyche" (Jung 1969b, p. 353). In other words, for both Heidegger and Jung we live *within* a world of revealed understandings.

To put this another way: There is an object in a room of my house with four protrusions extending downward to the floor from a flat surface. The meaning of this object for me lies in its presentation of itself as a place of work. On the flat surface, I spread out my tools—papers, pens, pencils, books, and word processor—and become immersed in a world of study and writing. In contrast, for my three-year-old son, the meaning of the same object is a fortress with covering overhead and four surrounding pillars from within which to carry on warfare with soldiers and guns, planes and bombs. For my wife, this same object becomes a vessel for relationship with candlelight and wine, a fine meal, and precious dinnerware. Three perceptions, three images, three meanings, three worlds—but within each world understanding, perception, and fantasy are all one.

Jung deepens our experience by giving *archetypal* significance to each realm. I am living in the world of Hephaestus, the holy smith of creative endeavor; my son in the world of Ares, a world of war and conflict, aggression, and defense; and my wife in a combined world of Aphrodite and Dionysus, where *eros* is created through a loosening of boundaries.[3]

Hillman perhaps helps us the most at this point:

> Psyche becomes aware by means of an imaginal method: the os-
> tentation of images, a parade of fantasies as imagination bodies
> forth its subtleties. *Nous* observer of *psyche*, seeing in her mirror
> how his mind actually proceeds. *Nous* at last psychological: all its
> cognitive instrumentarium become lunatic, the logic of images;
> psyche with logos. Here in the white earth psychology begins.
> (Hillman 1981, p. 52)

Now that we have a background of phenomenological sensibility and its connection with Jung, we can explore some of
Jung's foundational concepts—psyche, self, conscious/unconscious,
and archetype—to see that what at first appears as rational concept
prone to a reified, spiritualized sense of psychological life is, in
fact, grounded in experience. Whereas Jung tried to transcend
Cartesian dualism through an intuitive grasp of the workings of the
psyche, the logic of rationality in his language betrays his concealed sense of the *a priori* unity of body/psyche/world. The result
of the tension between the spirit of Jung's thought and the mode of
its expression is that the latter is undermined by tautologies, contradictions, and abstractions. The ontology of unification is still,
therefore, only an implicit promise in Jung's thought.

Psyche

Jung's experience in Africa illustrates his initial encounter with the
fundamental world-openness that phenomenologists call intentionality. This is a radical sense of the interactional nature of psyche
and world, and Brooke, himself a South African, sees Jung's account of his experience in Africa as an indication of his "recovery
of the world as the home of psychological life" (Brooke 1991, p.
57). Here Jung was taken by the event of the dawning of the light
of a new day which he suddenly grasped as a metaphor for "consciousness as the illuminating realm within which the being of the
world can shine forth" (ibid., p. 58). Jung intuited that meaning is
given in the metaphors through which the world speaks, was in-
delibly impressed by a "dawning significance of things"—sunrise,
jungle, animal, native man—and realized that through things the

world revealed itself as a "temple," without which there could be no reflective consciousness (Jung 1961, p. 268). "In Africa, Jung realized the self as a non-substantial openness within which the world could come into being" (Brooke 1991, p. 60). The longing for consciousness, then, is a longing for world, and it is through the world that consciousness dawns. It is misleading to speak of world *and* psyche, as Jungians often do; rather, each is a coconstitution of the other.

The notion of "psyche" needs not only a "world," however, but also a "body" in order to be rescued from the circularity of such definitions as "the totality of all psychic processes" (Jung 1971, p. 463). As we saw in chapter 2, phenomenology offers the position that what gives psychology body is an eye (or mind) that sees psyche as integral with the human body; indeed, psyche *is* the experience of the "lived body," or the place of existence "bodying forth." For phenomenology, all perception is bodily, hence in a sense unknowable, a mode of being "which is neither ego nor thing of the world" (Ricoeur 1970, p. 382). As Brooke paraphrases Merleau-Ponty, "what is loosely and misleadingly called the 'body,' provides density and limits to psychological life; (what is) loosely and misleadingly called the 'psyche' or 'mind' offers reflection and transcendence of (freedom from) the particularities that beset animal existence" (Brooke 1991, pp. 71–72).

Although Jung often wrote as though psyche were surrounded by body, he again intuitively sensed an *a priori* unity, this time between body and mind. In the Tavistock Lectures, Jung refers to body and mind as "two aspects of the living being" (1954, p. 34) and elsewhere concludes with "the mysterious truth that spirit is the life of the body seen from within, and the body, the outward manifestation of spirit—the two being really one" (1964, p. 94). Jung wrote, "The body is a visible expression of the here and now" (1976, p. 475). Thus, to talk of psyche *and* body is another misleading dualism imposed by rational language. In contrast, "to work with the depths of the psyche . . . is to reclaim those significances revealed within the lived body" (Brooke 1991, p. 69).

Brooke reformulates the Jungian sense of psyche as interior life, separate from outer world (a carryover from the age of Kant), into psyche as "life-world"—"the place of experience and that place is the world in which we live" (1991, p. 85). He points to three

ways in which Jung seems to have grasped in his own way the notion of life-world. First, as his writing on his experience in Africa
reveals, Jung could envision a *Weltanschauung* that rendered the
world as alive. Widened consciousness from this perspective is not
development of an interiorized psyche through self-reflection and
withdrawn projections as it is for the Kantian Jung but "is a function of relationship to the world of objects, bringing the individual
into absolute, binding and indissoluble communion with the world
at large" (Jung 1966b, p. 178). Second, through the notion of the
"psychoid," the hypothetical realm where spirit and matter come together, Jung was clearly attempting to bridge psyche and world. Finally, Jung's sense of the dialectical nature of analysis leads to a
sense of life-world as intersubjective; we are who we are only
through relationship.

Self

Jung, of course, regarded individuation as the central concept of
analytical psychology, and his positive view of individuation (in
contradistinction to Schopenhauer, who saw it as the consequence
of blind will) is intricately related to his notion of the self. Jung's
use of the notion of the self as a "center" or the "central archetype,"
which stems from the classical concept of proportion, forgets the
sense of *all* archetypes as centrally ordered and of many central aspects of psychic life as implicating each other. The self would be
seen by Brooke not as reified entity but as a *capacity* to structure
psychic life around a center. As totality, the self is the realization of
the ambiguity of existence known and unknown. Brooke emphasizes Jung's sense of the ontological unity between self and world
and cites Jung's statement: "Individuation does not shut one out
from the world but gathers the world to oneself" (Jung 1969b, p.
226). Individuation as the self's unfolding is the world's disclosure.
For Brooke, individuation as world-disclosiveness involves the
deliteralizing of one's engagements with the world into metaphorical structures. In the unfolding of self, we discover we are living a
story of which we are no longer the author. "I happen to myself"
(Jung 1969a, p. 259). With that discovery, we are able to experience
metaphor as the structuring element of our being. Individuation
then becomes "a process of differentiation and transformation in

which personal identity is established as an appropriation of a limited number of possible world disclosures and relationships from out of the totality of possibilities that Jung calls the self" (Brooke 1991, p. 119). In this sense of self, Brooke hears the echoes of Heidegger's *Dasein*.

> Like *Dasein*, the self is "mine" yet not personal; it is the embracing totality out of which individuality and identity emerge; it is realized at all levels of psychological development as a world with which one is engaged (even autistic flight is a kind of engagement); as a gathering of the world it brings the world into being in the light of human consciousness; it surrounds that place of identity one usually points to as "oneself," yet its spatiality is not extensive in the philosophical sense; it is a home within which the gods can be experienced and thought. (Brooke 1991, p. 106)

Consciousness and Unconsciousness

Any discussion of Jung's ontology has to address the apparent dualistic, static, and reified nature of Jung's definition of consciousness and unconsciousness. When he speaks of "contents" of the unconscious as if they (and it) were something literal or spatial and uses concepts of libido and compensation to describe the "dynamics" of the unconscious, Jung sounds like an Enlightenment philosopher taking a Cartesian, mechanistic view of the psyche. When he represents the unconscious in the ego's terms, he presents the psyche as a self-regulating system, a mechanical entity. This view serves the educational task of making the psyche accessible to the ego but at the loss of the ego's depth and complexity. On the other hand, when Jung allows himself to accept his own more radical *esse in anima*, he admits that consciousness is always more or less permeated with unconsciousness: "there is no conscious content which is not in some other respect unconscious" (Jung 1969b, p. 188).

From this relativistic position, Jung describes the unconscious as many particular modes of being in the world. "The unconscious" is not a psychic locality, again, not literal, but a vital matrix (which) discloses and gathers life-worlds that are at once primordial and historical and which have a life of their own that is lived but not known. It is an embodied, intentional ambiguousness, or rather, "a multitude of complex, (incarnate) intentionalities," a "presence that is present-as-an-absence," a face barely reflected, a voice dimly heard—calling for appropriation through the limitations of consciousness (Brooke 1991, pp. 126, 132).

Archetype

In considering the concept of the archetype, Brooke prefers to stress Jung's use of the term as a unifying concept, as when he speaks of archetypes as "categories of the *imagination*" (Jung 1969a, p. 518)—categories that are at once the sources of action, reaction, and experience. Archetypes *link* behavior and experience; behavior and attitude are coconstituted through the archetypal image. They are not static categories like museum holdings nor literal readings of personality gestalts; rather, the archetype must be seen in terms of its capacity for a gathering of situation/activity/attitude in a simultaneous, living structure. And again, archetypes as embodied through image are intricately linked to the world—"the human being's bodily potentialities which structure being-in-the-world in typically human ways" (Brooke 1991, p. 148).

In conclusion, phenomenology brings to Jung's writings a much-needed sensibility and a true encounter. It is a sensibility that is often paid lip service, but rarely reflected in the way Jungians think: that is, the coconstituting reality of world/psyche/body. Recently, Jungians have been scandalized by reference to Jungian psychology as a cult (Noll 1994). But through dogmatic allegiance to Jung's static, reified, mechanistic, and, at times, overly romantic nineteenth-century conceptualizations in formulating a "new culture," Jungians contribute to the notion of Jungian psychology as a quasi cult of spiritualized psychology. In their practice, when Jungians treat the individual as a character in a story that is given, forgetting that we create our world, and when they practice therapy as a "cult-ivation" of "inner life," mindless of context, leading the patient down the path of symbolic interpretation, isolated from personal history, daily events, family environment, or the vicissitudes of transference and countertransference, they are acting like priests rather than as therapists. In sum, if phenomenology needs Jungian psychology to realize the myth of experience in its full depth, it also points out Jungian psychology's condition as an Aegean stable in need of purgation of its deeply encrusted, overly spiritualized Cartesian ontology and provides a *solutio* for static conceptual structures that are, in fact, the discards of outworn philosophy, misplaced romanticism, and rampant dualism. Phenomenology and Jung are after the same thing—the union of mind/body/world in a psychological experience of "lived world" or "lived body," a unified state of participation in being.

4

THE TEMPLE OF DIONYSUS

DREAMS AS RELIGIOUS EXPERIENCE

"My friend, dreams are things hard to interpret, hopeless to puzzle out, and people find that not all of them end in anything."

—Homer, *The Odyssey*, xix.560–1

In his lectures entitled "Psychology and Religion," given in 1937 at Yale University, Jung attempted to demonstrate that the religious impulse is fundamental in the human psyche. Jung's sense of the constitutional basis of religion came in part from his family background and in part from his observations and research into the mythologies and religions of the world. In his lectures, Jung used a series of dreams of one of his patients to illustrate the religious nature of the psyche.

The first dream spoke of a ceremony in which an ape was to be reconstructed. Jung interprets this dream to indicate that a restructuring of the "instinctual personality," a form of spiritual "rebirth," is occurring in the dreamer's psyche.

The next dream went as follows.

All the houses have something theatrical about them, with stage scenery and decorations. The name of Bernard Shaw is mentioned. The play is supposed to take place in the distant future. There is a notice in English and German on one of the sets:

This is the universal Catholic Church.
It is the Church of the Lord.
All those who feel that they are the instruments of the Lord
may enter.

Under this is printed in smaller letters: "The Church was founded by
Jesus and Paul"—like a firm advertising its long standing.
I say to my friend, "Come on, let's have a look at this." He
replies, "I do not see why a lot of people have to get together when
they're feeling religious." I answer, "As a Protestant you will never
understand." A woman nods emphatic approval. Then I see a sort of
proclamation on the wall of the church. It runs:

Soldiers!

When you feel you are under the power of the Lord, do not address
him directly. The Lord cannot be reached by words. We also
strongly advise you not to indulge in any discussions among your-
selves concerning the attributes of the Lord. It is futile, for everything
valuable and important is ineffable.
(Signed) Pope . . . (Name illegible)

Now we go in. The interior resembles a mosque, more particularly
the Hagia Sophia: no seats—wonderful effect of space; no images,
only framed texts decorating the walls (like the Koran texts in the
Hagia Sophia). One of the texts reads "Do not flatter your benefac-
tor." The woman who had nodded approval bursts into tears and
cries, "Then there's nothing left!" I reply, "I find it quite right!" but
she vanishes. At first I stand with a pillar in front of me and can see
nothing. Then I change my position and see a crowd of people. I do
not belong to them and stand alone. But they are quite clear, so that
I can see their faces. They all say in unison, "We confess that we are
under the power of the Lord. The Kingdom of Heaven is within us."
They repeat this three times with great solemnity. Then the organ
starts to play and they sing a Bach fugue with chorale. But the orig-
inal text is omitted; sometimes there is only a sort of coloratura
singing, then the words are repeated: "Everything else is paper"
(meaning that it does not make a living impression on me). When
the chorale has faded away the gemütlich part of the ceremony

begins; it is almost like a students' party. The people are all cheerful and equable. We move about, converse, and greet one another, and wine (from an episcopal seminary) is served with other refreshments. The health of the Church is drunk and, as if to express everybody's pleasure at the increase in membership, a loudspeaker blares a ragtime melody with the refrain, "Charles is also with us now." A priest explains to me: "These somewhat trivial amusements are officially approved and permitted. We must adapt a little to American methods. With a large crowd such as we have here this is inevitable. But we differ in principle from the American churches by our decidedly anti-ascetic tendency." Thereupon I awake with a feeling of great relief.

Jung interprets the dream to be "an impartial statement of the patient's spiritual condition . . . (raising) the problem of a religious attitude" (Jung 1969a, p. 32). He asserts that the intrusion of pagan revels into the solemnity of the Catholic ritual indicates a "compromise" in the dreamer's conscious attitude toward religion. The dream "gives a picture of a degenerate religion corrupted by worldliness and mob instincts. There is religious sentimentality instead of the *numinosum* of divine experience" (ibid.). Jung concludes that the church dream is "definitely unfavorable," reflecting an attempt by the dreamer to escape unconscious fears of immediate religious experience.

Jung depicts a subsequent dream as an indication that the patient's attitude toward religion has taken a turn. In this dream, the dreamer enters a solemn house. He listens to a voice proclaiming the necessity of taking into account "the other side of the soul's life" in order to inhabit a truly religious attitude. The other side of the soul's life is declared to be "the woman's image" or, for Jung, the anima, the feminine aspect of the male psyche. From this view the anima would represent the patient's emotional life, which has been neglected. Jung takes the dream to be a message from the unconscious saying,

> You try religion in order to escape from your unconscious. You use it as a substitute for a part of your soul's life. But religion is the fruit and culmination of the completeness of life, that is of a life which contains both sides. (Ibid., p. 42)

In sum, Jung interprets the content of the dream to be calling for a change in the conscious attitude of the dreamer toward his unconscious "feminine" side. This change in consciousness has religious overtones which are fearful to the dreamer.

Whereas Freud considered religion an illusion, Jung saw an intricate connection between religion and psychic reality. For Jung, modern man overemphasized his reasoning faculty, giving rise to a view of reality as exterior and material at the expense of spiritual life. At the same time, religion had lost its vitality through its institutionalization. The result was that modern man had become a neurotic, half-living creature, cut off from instinctual life and in search of soul. Jung located the lost soul of modern man in the interior personality, the unconscious, and saw its representatives in the form of dreams and fantasies. In dreams one could find the remnants of instinctual and spiritual life that had been buried under layers of institutional religious dogma and rationalist thought. The psychologist as archaeologist and historian of religion needed to be able to interpret the language of the psyche to discover its hidden religious stratum.

In "Psychology and Religion," Jung attempted to stake a claim for the psychological reality of religious life. He did so by presenting the view that all of actual experience is a matter of psychological reality. Experience is empirical regardless of whether or not it can be publicly observed, measured, and repeated; thus religious experience is just as valid as any other.

Religious experience for Jung is the "careful and scrupulous observation" of the *numinosum* or that higher power which "seizes and controls" the human subject (Jung 1969a, p. 7). In other words, it is the experience of a "dynamic agency," independent of subjective will that causes an alteration in consciousness. Religion is an "attitude of mind" that honors the "original experience," of that which is "powerful," "dangerous," "helpful," "grand," "beautiful," and "meaningful" (ibid., pp. 7–8). It is an experience that is accorded the "highest value" regardless of its contents (ibid., p. 62).

The life of religion, that is, the meaningful experience of something more powerful than ourselves, "the feeling for the infinite" (Jung 1961, p. 325), is a potential we all carry. However, it is fearsome and hence obscured by psychophysical defenses. It finds its expression in the "cancerous tumors" of the body and mind, literal cancer and neurotic symptoms. Through dis-ease we experience the gods (Jung 1967, p. 37).

There is another source of expression for transcendent power: dreams. "Dreams are the voice of the Unknown" revealing "the unknown inner facts of the psyche" (Jung 1969a, pp. 18, 23). As the voice of the unknown, dreams give expression to that which has been forgotten, including genuine religious experience.

Dreams have always been associated with the divine. For the ancient Babylonians, Egyptians, and Greeks, dreams were messages from the gods, declaring the will of the gods and connecting the human world with the divine. The Egyptians even had a god for dreams, Bes, whose head was carved on wooden pillows. In these traditions, illness and cure came from the god through dreams. If the god who caused the disease appeared in celestial or animal form in the dream, the dreamer would be cured. Some native tribes such as the Uitoto of Colombia and some Australian bush tribes imagine all waking life as emanating from the dreamed life of the gods. For them, dreams are reality.

Whereas Jung speaks of dreams as being *about* religion, in the traditions of antiquity and certain native peoples, dreams can also be taken as religious experience itself. In this chapter, I would like to regain the sense of dreams themselves as religious events in that they allow for the experience of an autonomous realm that encompasses the subjective mind. With this attitude, we lose the certainty and comfort of the subjectivist position that distances itself from the dream and sees it as object to be interpreted for the sake of meaning. On the other hand, if we remain on exactly that psychological ground that Jung staked out, we would honor the dream on its own terms, entering into it as a religious happening in its own right. From this perspective, Jung considered the entry to the dream to be the dream image itself, which contains its own configurations of meaning independent of systems of interpretation. In sum, I will be attempting to connect the religious and aesthetic stances through an imaginal vision of the dream.

James Hillman (1979b) helps us formulate the particular religious nature of dreams. He points out that religious experience is not only the experience of powers of spirit (pneuma) but also the experience of soul (psyche). Heraclitus locates soul in the depths: "You could not discover the limits of the soul, even if you traveled every road to do so, such is the depth of its meaning" (Wheel-wright 1964, p. 58).[1] The mythical realm of depth is the under-world, and the underworld is associated with dreams. Homer imagines dreams as personages living on the path to the under-world, and Hermes, the mythical bringer of sleep and dreams, was also the guide to and from the underworld. The underworld is ruled by the invisible god, Hades, who is experienced as coming into our lives uninvited and who takes us into a mode of percep-tion that is like death to the naïveté of the ego's literalism and ra-tional clarity. This sense of the underworld as a place where perception is radically different from waking life is reflected in the Egyptian notion of the underworld as a place where everything ex-ists upside down, the opposite of its day-world correlate.

A second way of delineating the realm of dreams as a place of soul is the perspective of "night world." According to Hesiod, the mother of dreams is night. Night is a "world in itself" (Otto 1979, p. 118), a place of ambiguity, paradox, strangeness, and mystery akin to the experience of dreams. Night consciousness is a form of limi-nal consciousness, betwixt and between, or a twilight zone where the rationalist split between subject and object no longer holds. It is consciousness where the control, certainty, and intentionality of the subjective mind is lost, where things take on a life and will of their own.

Finally, dreams are traditionally associated with the realm of the dead. Hesiod imagines sleep and death to be brothers, so that dreaming would be a form of death in life. In the ancient Egyptian mind, the soul of the sleeper enters the realm of the dead through which the sun god, Ra, makes a nocturnal journey from west to east, finally emerging renewed as the rising sun in the mouth of a dragon.[2]

Whereas Freud talks about religion as a defense and Jung talks about religious creed as a defense from the "immediate reli-gious experience," Hillman asserts that the rational view of dreams (as disguise of unconscious thought—Freud; as compensation of unconscious attitude—Jung) is a defense against the immediate ex-perience of the dream. The view of the dream from the perspective of the underworld, night world, and realm of the dead helps us de-velop a consciousness that allows for a more direct "animal per-ception" of the dream (Hillman 1979a). If we are to know the dream as an experience, then we will need to "abandon all hope" (Dante's phrase upon entering the Inferno) for rational meaning, clarity, and certainty.

The underworld mythically is a realm to be entered for the sake of learning what can't be known in the world above, and the heroic effort to take something from the underworld is usually frustrated. So our need to take meaning from the dream, to use the dream to give direction to our day-world confusions, even to consider dreams as having value in our lives, is a need in the service of a spiritual yearning that does not honor the particularity of the actual experience of the dream, the experience of soul—the underworld, the night world, the realm of death. Rather than seeing the dream through day-world conceptual structures ("I had a dream"), the dream itself would be seen as a religious experience that has us, an initiatory journey into a realm of transformed consciousness. For example, the dream would not be seen so much as a tool to be used to enhance life, but as a process of death for all of us every night. Finally, dreams would be seen to be working on us, in-forming us so that our day-world consciousness would become more dreamlike, more precise in its perception of "shades" (an underworld form), less literal; and our experience of our self more that of the many different selves we encounter in the dream.

Precisely how can we approach the dream in a way that honors its particular underworldly, religious nature? Depth psychology has struggled with this question throughout its short history, and it might be helpful to examine briefly its differing points of view.

Freud makes a distinction between the expressions of the waking state and those of the dream state. Following Schleiermacher, Freud asserts that "what characterizes the waking state is the fact that thought-activity takes place in *concepts* and not in *images*" (Freud 1965a, p. 82). Waking life is characterized by rationality, thoughts, and concepts, while dreams express themselves through images. "[D]reams, then, think predominantly in visual images" (ibid.). Here, Freud is taking the phenomenological stance of imputing subjectivity to the dream itself but also, from the rational standpoint, assigning it to an inherently inferior mode connected with the "regressive" (ibid., p. 581), childlike (ibid., p. 224), and "archaic" (Freud 1952, p. 189). The dream image is a mere "facade" with which "we would concern (ourselves) as little as possible" (Freud 1965b, p. 10). Freud's image of psychological dynamics, based on nineteenth-century laws of hydromechanics, was that the apparatus of the psyche transformed thoughts that were unacceptable to consciousness into irrational images that were acceptable ("pouring the content of a thought into another mould"—Freud 1965a, p. 379).[3]

In sum, for Freud, the valuable aspect of dream life is that part associated with waking life, the dream thoughts, which lie latent in the unconscious until they appear in disguised form as dream images. The dream is caused by experiences from waking life that stimulate thoughts which are unacceptable to waking consciousness. Freud is clear in his intention for dream analysis, that is, to undo the expression of the night world (images) and turn them into expressions of waking life (thoughts) for the sake of deriving meaning through scientific methodology.

> The aim which I have set before myself is to show that dreams are capable of being interpreted . . . "Interpreting" a dream implies assigning a "meaning" to it . . . . A scientific procedure for interpreting (dreams) is possible. (Freud 1965a, pp. 128, 132)

The task of the analyst, ever suspicious of the dream image, is to "demolish" the edifice of the dream in order to find a latent, rational truth (Freud 1952, p. 179). It is the system of interpretation that is important, not the thing in itself, the dream image. Freud's system of interpretation provides an aggressive movement through the dream as "royal road to the unconscious," exposing the secrets of the night world and restoring the rational grammar of waking life.

Jung's thought on dreams can be shown to hold an ambiguity that parallels Freud's distinction between sleeping and waking consciousness. Jung's ambivalence toward what he referred to as the "nocturnal realm of the psyche" (Jung 1966a, p. 151) can be seen in his description of the dream as a *"spontaneous self-portrayal, in symbolic form, of the actual situation in the unconscious"* (Jung 1969b, p. 263). "Spontaneous self-portrayal . . . of the actual situation in the unconscious" implies the display of an image that holds its own meaning. This sense of the revealing nature of the dream stands in opposition to Freud, who saw the dream as concealing the actual situation. The revealing is only approximate, however, for it is still in "symbolic form," requiring interpretation. The unconscious is speaking its own language, and it requires the ability of one with "sense and ingenuity to read the enigmatic message from the nocturnal realm of the psyche" (Jung 1966a, p. 151). Jung is making way for an understanding of the dream based on a system of interpretation of something unknown. What Jung doesn't take into account, however, is that the meaning of the dream image will depend on the system of interpretation or the attitudes and preconceptions toward the unconscious held by the interpreter (Berry 1974).

When Jung approaches the dream through a rational system, he is operating within the theoretical framework of oppositions. In this case, the opposition is between conscious and unconscious. Jung poses the concept of compensation as the relation between the two. The dream is a factor generated by the unconscious in compensation for a conscious attitude. In other words, manifestations of the unconscious—the dream images—must be regarded with an eye to something else—the conscious attitude of the dreamer.

> If we want to interpret a dream correctly, we need a thorough knowledge of the conscious situation at that moment, because the dream contains its unconscious complement, that is, the material which the conscious situation has constellated in the unconscious. (Jung 1969b, pp. 248–249).

> Since the meaning of most dreams is not in accord with the tendencies of the conscious mind but shows peculiar deviations, we must assume that the unconscious, the matrix of dreams, has an independent function . . . When I attempted to express this behavior in a formula the concept of *compensation* seemed to me the only adequate one . . . Compensation . . . as the term implies, means balancing and comparing different data or points of view so as to produce an adjustment or a rectification. (Jung 1969b, p. 287)

Jung's metapsychology of opposites rests on an ontology of wholeness or symmetry, not unlike the classic metaphysics of proportion. The dream is a product of the total psyche in that it serves to balance one part of the whole with another. For Jung, the tendency of the psyche is toward an equivalence in energy charges between consciousness and unconsciousness, an idea based on the first and second laws of thermodynamics which state that energy in a system seeks a state of equilibrium. Here, Jung is on the same ontological ground as Freud in approaching the dream. He has a preconception of a source of meaning (Freud—unconscious thoughts; Jung—totality of the psyche), associates the dream with a distortion of or deviation from this source, and employs a system or formula for bringing about the rectification.

In the dreams of his patient, through the lens of his own conceptual formulations of "masculine" and "feminine," Jung saw a process of correction of a conscious attitude. According to Jung, the dreamer was overly influenced by a traditional, "masculine" orientation at the expense of an inner, unconscious "feminine" counterpart of his personality. Jung interpreted the dream as making a moral statement expressing the need for the dreamer to give himself over to a genuine religious attitude which would start with honoring the feminine side of his nature. It is not the dream, rather it is Jung who is the moralist.

Jung's perception of the voice in the third dream as "a basic religious phenomenon" gives a clue as to a different approach to the dream (Jung 1969a, p. 39). From this position, Jung honors the dream image itself without the use of a system of interpretation involving concepts of masculine and feminine. Jung writes,

> The dream is a little hidden door in the innermost and most secret recesses of the soul, opening into that cosmic night which was psyche long before there was any ego consciousness, and which will remain psyche no matter how far our ego consciousness may extend. (1970, pp. 144–45)

In following Heraclitus's sense of soul as encompassing our attempts to measure it, Jung is approaching the dream in a psychological manner by declining the spiritual intention of deriving meaning. Dream as "doorway" accepts the dream on its own terms without taking an interpretive trip down a "royal road." One can see through a door and pass through it as one can see through and enter into an image. The dream is no longer an object for the subjective mind to derive meaning from or utilize, but a realm to be entered into and in-formed by as religious experience.

As we have noted, Freud considered "image" to be the mode of expression of the sleeping state, as opposed to "concept," the mode of expression of the waking state, and held the latter to be the receptacle of meaning. In contrast, from his aesthetic stance Jung wrote, "Image and meaning are identical and as the first takes shape, so the latter becomes clear" (1969b, p. 204). As we saw in chapters 1 and 3, Jung considered image as the ground of psyche— "every psychic process is an image" (1969a, 544); "image is psyche" (1967, p. 50). Further, Jung locates the immediacy of life, echoing the immediacy of religious experience, in our ability to sense images: "images . . . alone constitute my immediate experience" (1969b, p. 353). From the aesthetic position, then, Jung is saying that the dream image itself holds the meaning we seek. To understand its meaning, he would "stick as close as possible to the dream images" (1966a, p. 149). Jung concludes,

> So the dream presents an impartial truth. It shows the situation which by law of nature is. It does not say you ought to do this or that, nor does it say what is good or bad. It simply shows the dreamer in a situation. Man is so underneath. This is the truth. (Quoted in McGuire 1984, p. 204)

In these passages, image and meaning, appearance and truth are united. No systems of proportion, harmony, opposition, or compensation are called for in order to elucidate meaning. Appearance itself is all that is necessary when perceived through the aesthetic eye unmediated by concept.

The dream comes to us on its own terms, psychic images, and for us to meet the dream, we have to consider it on aesthetic ground. Image is not only what is seen, but a way of seeing, a way of seeing that reflects an attitude of mind that honors something as more than itself. Images are religious in that we are seized by them and held by them. They are larger than us, a world of powers beyond that of the subjective will. No value judgments or moral lessons are implied from the dream. Nor is the dream to be seen as indicating a preferred way of being in the day world or giving advice for action to take in daily life. Rather, the dream image is to be seen as the presentation of a world in itself. Honoring the religious nature of the dream, then, is to see it through its own image. This would not be a passive undisciplined or ecstatic endeavor, but a contemplative process of entering into the dream image and deepening its experience. The work of Patricia Berry (1974), James Hillman (1977, 1978, 1979a, 1979b), and Robert Bosnak (1988, 1996) help us in this enterprise.

Berry teaches us that when we analyze an image we are considering something simultaneous in time and intrarelational in space. No part of the dream precedes another, nor is there a causal relationship between parts of the dream or between daily life and the dream. Each part of the dream is related and inseparable in time, correlative and contemporaneous, all parts going on at the same time. Berry suggests we approach the dream in terms of "when–then"—when this part of the dream occurs, then that part also occurs, two parts of the psyche acting in conjunction. She proposes that an aesthetic stance toward the dream image involves a contemplative process of repetition and restating. Each section of the dream is read and reread, deepened by hearing and rehearing the reverberations of its undertones and overtones. This approach allows for the emergence of the metaphor in the images. Questions in relation to the dream would be not so much, "What does this mean in life?" but, "What is this like in life?"—a process the early church fathers called "seeing the likeness in images" (Miller 1980, p. 85).

In "On Psychology and Religion," Jung talks about the god Dionysus as amplification of the party atmosphere in the church. Elsewhere, Jung alludes to Dionysus in postulating a dramatic structure for the dream—setting, development, *peripeteia*, *lysis* (1969b, pp. 294–295). Although Jung's attitude toward Dionysus is pejorative in the first case, and the dramatic structure does not adhere to the actual dream experience, a consideration of Dionysus does reveal him to be a god in the background of a religious approach to dreams. Dionysus is Lord of Souls, *zoe*, the god of comings and goings of life force, taking us back to our religious origins. Heraclitus considers Dionysus and Hades as equivalents, indicating the underworldly nature of Dionysian experience. In the dream as in the underworld, personages, settings, and events become like shades or shadows reflected in the masks of ancient Dionysian pageants. Likewise, Dionysian logic sees any personage or thing in the dream as but one perspective in the constant flow of available perceptions offered by the dream. Thus Hillman suggests nothing can be literally "true," there can be no "bottom line," no single meaning from the Dionysian perspective (Hillman 1975a, p. 160). Dionysus as the child god, perpetually dis-membered and re-membered, is echoed by Freud ("we find the child and the child's impulses still living on in the dream"— Freud 1965a, p. 224) and manifests in our experience of dreams as dispersing and needing to be remembered. Rather than having an Apollonian structure, dreams are experienced more immediately as fragmentation in accordance with Dionysus as the "great loosener," or the "mad god," and reflected in Freud's association of dreams with psychosis (1965b, p. 16).

The Dionysian *logos* or form that fits the dream is not a fixed structure but a liminal experience of the merging of subject and object. Dionysus tears down the inner/outer distinctions that allow for our day-world sense of certainty and control. Likewise, the dream is a presentation of figures, things, and events that participate in both inner and outer world simultaneously and yet not in either one completely, neither objective nor subjective. The "I" in the dream both is and is not the "I" of daily life. As Dionysian experience, "the dream is not a coded message at all but a display, a *Schau,* in which the dreamer himself plays a part or is in the audience and thus always involved" (Hillman 1975a, p. 160).

Dionysian dream logic that relativizes the conscious ego is further helped by two contributors to dream theory, Fritz Perls and Medard Boss. Perls, the outstanding spokesman for Gestalt therapy, sees every part of the dream, animate and inanimate, as a part of the dreamer. In working with dreams, Perls has the dreamer create dialogues between different parts of the dream; the ceiling may talk with the floor, just as the victim may talk with the perpetrator, each part having coequal importance. On the other hand, Boss, a spokesman for existential analysis, considers dreams as depicting ways of being in the world, how we are "thrown into a world" (1977, p. 8). In other words, we are not personalities as nouns so much as we are verbs and adverbs.

> We occur as nothing other than a world-spanning, open reposing domain that is an ability to perceive, an ability to be addressed by encountered things, and an ability to answer . . . . We are nothing other than receptive, alert world-disclosiveness. We have to exist

as such a world disclosiveness in order to be claimed. (Boss 1977, p. 9)

In other words, there can be no "inner" without an "outer" in contrast. We exist as perceiving and answering relationships with things. In working with dreams, the existentialist will ask the dreamer questions about how the dream displays an image of the way in which the dreamer is open to and cocreates the world.

To conclude by going back to the dreams of Jung's patient, the dreams are seen somewhat differently from the religious, aesthetic, existential standpoint than from the standpoint of metapsychology, which sees in them a moral statement by the unconscious. Following Hillman (1979a), rather than regarding the ape as a symbol to be interpreted as "instinctual personality," the ape would be regarded as an imaginal animal, a revealed presence. The psychological questions would be, What is the ape like? What does it want of the dreamer? Why is it appearing now? Why an ape and not a bird or a snake? What is being "aped" in the dreamer's life?

When addressed aesthetically (Hillman 1979a), the second dream seems to emphasize "play" (theatrical houses, Bernard Shaw, play to take place in the future, people as "instruments" of the Lord, "long-standing run" of the Catholic Church). Play has a religious quality and religion can be playful (Miller 1973). The tone of the dream upon entering the home seems to be the giving over of control to an unknown power ("feeling religious," "under the power of the Lord . . . (who) cannot be reached by words," "everything valuable and important is ineffable," unknown Pope) that expresses through words (a notice, a proclamation, framed texts). Or is this an image of word power or the play of words or the divinity in language (Lockhart 1983)?

When the woman cries, the benefactor is flattered. She is opposed to flattery, but there is nothing left from her perspective. When the dreamer shifts his perspective, a crowd appears, but he is alone in facing them. They are confessing to be under the power of the Lord. In singing coloratura are they being played by the Lord? Who is the Lord here? What are the colors in the dreamers life? Organ play is godly. Is that because masturbation brings fantasy? Only when the singing fades away can the mixing begin with wine and toasting. Not in formal time but in "rag time" can the dreamer join the group and be impressed by the religiosity of the occasion. What is it to be a "rag picker"?

In short, the dream seems to be a ritual in itself portraying the transformation of isolation and distance to relationship and involvement. From the standpoint of the dream, there is nothing to indicate a problem, and such an interpretation would only indicate Jung's preconceptions regarding the form of the religious attitude. Likewise, the final dream can be seen not so much as a moralizing sermon that indicates what the dreamer must do in his life but a ritual, which in itself gathers (candles burning in four-pointed pattern, people collecting themselves) the different actions of the soul in flux reflected by the flame of the burning mountain.

Jung wrote, "Whenever we speak of religious contents we move in a world of images that point to something ineffable" (1969a, p. 360). The dream of his patient initiates Jung into the perception of the dream itself as a space of religious experience. In this chapter, we further Jung's insights by bringing together the religious and aesthetic ontological positions through the medium of the imagination. Hillman considers image to be "the grand conjunction of body, soul, and spirit" (1979a, p. 142). I am suggesting that the dream is where we have access to this conjunction, and that only through the plastic and dynamic elements of imagination are we able to meet this experience in full engagement. By taking the subjective position that we can derive meaning or use from dreams, we lose their ineffable, "larger than" nature. Just as the Bible is a "baffling compound of realistic element, incredible episodes and mythical categories" (Wilder 1976, p. 106), so the dream, as a "chamber of imagery" (Ezekiel 8:12), is full of epiphanies, rituals, and "upside-down events" from which we are removed by the interpretive mode. Jung: "One does not dream, one is dreamt. We 'suffer' the dream; we are its objects" (quoted in Jacobi 1973, p. 73).

5

SHIPWRECKS AND DICETHROWS

THE ERRANCY OF ANALYSIS

The Tragic Fool

I would like to start with the image of the tragic fool of the Middle Ages. We usually think of the fool as being a jester, undermining the hero or mocking the king. The wise fool in *King Lear* turns Lear's rigid inflation upside down, revealing the authority of the fool and the folly at work in blind authority. The holy fool can be seen in the mudhead tricksters of southwest Native American rituals who taunt the heroic kachina or shalako dancers and subsequently dance along beside them, chaos and order finding their inherent connection. Fools for Christ turn the notion of fool upside down by portraying God's ways as foolish from the standpoint of nonbelievers.

V. A. Kolve (1984) has discerned another kind of fool in medieval biblical iconography, a tragic or godless fool. Medieval illustrators depicted this figure as a sort of madman with a grotesque bearing—wearing torn garments, twisting his body into contorted positions, gnawing at fruit, and engaging in savage mockery of Jesus, even participating in his crucifixion. In the presence of Jesus, he utters, "*non es deus.*" Kolve found this icon associated with passages in the Book of Psalms, which say that the kingdom of God includes even those who negate God.

Kolve speculates that the medieval church fathers, following in the tradition of Augustine, would have thought that only a person deficient in reason, such as a fool, would deny God's existence. God, in turn, would benevolently tolerate even those who denied his existence and welcome them into His Kingdom. From the Christian standpoint, he who denies God is a fool, but God will love even a fool.

The traditional Western metaphysical structure of being is that behind each appearance lies its meaning. What presents itself at hand emanates from a source of higher authority. We can see this in science, for example, where truth is discerned not from experience but from statistical analysis of many observations. Contemporary deconstruction presents an alternative ontology. The deconstructionist's view is that Western consciousness has been stifled by its presupposition that presence exists in the action of speech (with writing as a derivative of speech). In Western metaphysics, self exists through the power of speech to align the speaker with meaning. Meaning is assumed to be present to the speaker through an intuitive act of self-surveillance that ensures a conjoining of intention and utterance. For the deconstructionist, this meaning is an illusion, a form of nostalgic yearning for a logocentric source (god). The only presence is the literary functioning of the mind from which all sense of self is derived. Deconstruction acts as the tragic fool to the traditional Western metaphysical structure of being.

Jesus the Deconstructionist

Ironically, from a theological standpoint, Jesus himself can be seen as a fool, sabotaging traditional authority and undermining the comfort of alignment or identification with dogmatic authority through his radical iconoclastic use of language. Jesus was faced with the Jewish spiritual tradition, which did not allow for graven images. God's form was thought to be unimaginable by humans (Isaiah 40:18, 25); He could not be trapped in image. John Dominic Crossan raises the question, Could not a god-form be hidden in the structure of speech itself? Crossan asks, "Might there not be an idolatry of forms and images made by minds just as easily as there could be such for forms and images made by hands?" (1976, p. 56). If this were the case, asserts Crossan, Jesus would be iconoclastic in undermining the structures that allow for alignment with God as authority rather than forcing an individual recognition of God in the experience of the moment. Thus, "Jesus represents the full flowering of Israel's aniconic faith, the consummate creativity of Israel's iconoclastic imagination" (ibid., p. 60).

From a deconstructionist standpoint, institutionalized language structure assumes a godlike meaning as a referent behind words. In this sense, language names, represents, patterns, combines, connects, and disconnects things as it makes them visible in the transparency of words. Through one-to-one representation (structure), signifier to signified, meaning (god) is evoked. Crossan sees Jesus working against spiritual tradition as embodied in structured language by evoking the limits of words and word forms through paradox and parable. Jesus works against the underlying assumption that to be with God is to follow rules of dogma or institution by identifying with authority implied in the structure of institutional language. By using parable and paradox, Jesus is saying that God cannot be fixed by us, even as we try to do so in the structure of our language. Jesus presents himself as the tragic fool, standing outside of and undermining the traditional order which gives the ego comfort in its delusion of alignment with the divine.

Crossan's thesis is that what Jesus might have said is one thing; how Jesus' sayings were interpreted by the gospel writers and the Christian tradition is something else. He suggests that while Jesus was actually undermining a monolithic language structure through paradox, his disciples recorded him in such a way as to suit their need for coherence with a spiritual tradition of logic. Crossan asserts that the paradoxical idea, "to him who has will be given, and from him who has not will be taken away," is distorted in Biblical text. Matthew expressed this idea as

> For unto every one that hath shall be given, and he shall have abundance: but from him that hath not shall be taken away even that which he hath. (25:29)

Likewise, Luke wrote:

> For I say unto you, That unto every one which hath shall be given; and from him that hath not, even that he had shall be taken away from him. (19:26)

Mark's version is,

> For he that hath, to him shall be given: and he that hath not from
> him shall be taken even that which he hath. (4:25)

Jesus' disciples and subsequent interpreters have tried to make logical sense of Jesus' irrational thought pattern by adding such phrases as "and he will have abundance" to the main theme, "to him who has will be given." Likewise, to the paradoxical thought "from him who has not will be taken away" is added "he from whom something is taken *must* have had something and even that will be taken away." Crossan argues that these additions diverge from the iconoclastic intention of Jesus' language wherein he gives a double paradox that thwarts the rational mind.

Similarly, the idea—who gains his life, loses it; who loses his life, gains it—is rendered by the gospel writers so as to make rational sense. Matthew:

> He that findeth his life shall lose it: and he that loseth his life for
> my sake shall find it. (10:39)

Mark:

> For whosoever will save his life shall lose it; but whosoever shall
> give his life for my sake and the gospel's, the same shall save it.
> (8:35)

Luke:

> Whosoever shall seek to save his life shall lose it and whosoever
> shall lose his life shall preserve it. (17:33)

John:

> He that loveth his life shall lose it; and he that hateth his life in
> this world shall keep it unto life eternal. (12:25)

Crossan asserts that Jesus is not talking about "for my sake" or "the future life" or "eternal life," but instead, through paradox, Jesus is undermining the comfort of alignment with authority of the *logos*, the word, and leaving the listener to wrestle with the chaos of actual experience. He who gains, loses; he who loses, gains.

Likewise, the beatitudes are diminished in force by a similar misreading. Luke relates the first beatitude as

> Blessed be ye poor: for your's is the kingdom of God. (6:20)

Matthew's version is

> Blessed are the poor in spirit: for their's is the kingdom of heaven. (5:3)

He later adds time and place qualifiers: if you are poor now, on earth, then in the future, in heaven, there will be reward. Luke makes this explicit:

> Rejoice ye in that day, and leap for joy for behold your reward is great in heaven. (6:22)

Crossan reminds us, however, that Jesus said simply: blessed the poor; their's is the kingdom. Jesus doesn't promise anything but leaves us with a dark, complex, multifaceted reality.

Jesus' sense of paradox leads us into a place of "difficult beauty" (Crossan 1976, p. 73). It is uncomfortable, dark, and unbalanced. We are forced to stop and reflect, to rethink our presuppositions. Crossan points out that Jesus tells the parable of the good samaritan as a Jewish narrator talking to a Jewish audience. In the story, a Jewish man was not helped by his own kind but was helped by an enemy. Was he giving an example of righteous action? No, rather he was saying, "Stop! Wake up!" using paradox to provoke his audience out of a lethargy of consciousness, a morass of identification with common assumptions.

Likewise, the parable of the vineyard, wherein a man goes out at different times during the day, hires idlers for work, and then gives them all the same amount of money, jolts our customary assumptions. It doesn't seem fair! We want to make this about democracy, goodness, and generosity, but it is about surprise and the reversal of expectations that come about in undermining the structures hidden in language itself. There is no external authority upon which to fall back to give a sense of presence. Through the uncertainty of language we are being taught the uncertainty of being.

The parable opens us up to imagination and invites imagination to a reversal of expectations. It opens the imagination to
multiple levels, many ways of seeing and interpreting so that one
can't rely on assumed presence or authority of source or origin behind words. As we are about to find out, we are thrown back into
the space of language itself, the "domed," uncertain worlds within
words.

>   I am
>   aware
> of them, as you must be, or you will miss
>
> the non-song
>
> in my singing: it is not that words *cannot* say
> what is missing: it is only that what is missing
>   cannot
>   be missed if
> spoken: read the parables of my unmaking:
>
> feel the ris-
>
> ing bubble's trembling walls: rush into the domes
> their wordy arches shape: hear
>   me
>   when I am
> silent: gather the boundaried vacancies.

>   (from "Unsaid," Ammons 1972, p. 91)

Odysseus's Shipwreck

We are imagining language as the foundation of our being and finding that built into Western language structure is the metaphysical assumption that words refer to an invisible meaning or source that lies
beyond the immediate signifier. We derive our sense of presence by
aligning ourselves with that meaning or source through using words
as signifiers in service to us. When this structure is undermined, then
our notion of presence or self is also undermined.

We have seen two images for this event in the tragic fool
and in Jesus' use of paradoxical language. A third image emerges
from a deconstructionist view of Dante's encounter with the hero

Odysseus in the *Inferno*. Dante is being led through the under-world by his guide, Virgil. In Dante's imagination, the Inferno is in-habited by sinners, many of whom can be seen to represent a particular abuse of language. Each sinner is punished with the mode of abuse they performed in their earthly life. When the trav-elers find themselves beside a ditch of flames, they are in the realm of false counselors, those who have used burning oration with tongues of flame to persuade others toward their own purposes.

Odysseus emerges as one of these flames and converses with Virgil. He tells how, after he left Circe, his passion to gain ex-perience drove him to exhort his band of men to journey to the outer reaches of the world, beyond where men had ever gone and where they met their ultimate doom in shipwreck. This passage is usually read as an indication of Odysseus's use of rhetorical per-suasion to serve his private end. The punishment for this abuse is to suffer the heat of language as an agent of damnation. Odysseus, possessed by the power of language in his life, is trapped by the fire of his own tongue in the afterlife.

An alternate view of this story is suggested by Giuseppe Mazzotta (1979), who makes the point that Dante is revealing not so much Odysseus's fraudulent use of language but the fraudulent nature of language itself. Language is shifty, ambiguous, and seduc-tive, exactly those qualities attributed to Odysseus. While language appears to create and organize the world, words as signifiers point-ing to signified meaning, in fact it conceals the world. Odysseus in mad flight tries to traverse the gap between signifier and signified, to attain that place beyond human knowing where word and meaning come together. His inferred intention is to arrive at the ori-gin or source of meaning, beyond speech, where there is no gap between referent and referred, hence no need of representation. This is the place of no sign and no signified, where ultimate mean-ing is immediately grasped.

From the deconstructionistic view, Odysseus's confusion was to regard language as the vehicle with which to traverse the gap between experience and meaning rather than to see the inher-ently uncertain quality of language. Language can't be a vehicle for transcending the world because it only reflects what is unknowable and intrinsically ambivalent. In other words, language is a world it-self, or the world is a reflection of language. Meaning is already at hand in language, so that no interpretive voyage to meaning is necessary. To deny this uncertainty leads to a perpetual yearning for transcendent meaning beyond the horizon, which in turn leads to inevitable shipwreck.

French Symbolism

The image of consciousness as a voyage of language emerges again three hundred years after Dante in the poems of the French symbolists. Charles Baudelaire envisioned existence as a gap or interval between the mundane and the ideal. This gap is an abyss, a swirl of ennui, and a desire to journey from the mundane to the spiritual is evoked.

> —Alas! All is abyss! Desire, act, dream,
> Word! . . . .
> Above, below, around me, shores descending . . .
> Silence . . . frightful, captivating Space. . . .
>
> My spirit, always haunted now by slumber,
> Yearns for extinction, insensibility. . . .
>
> (from "The Abyss," Baudelaire 1955, p. 147–149)

The true journey is not a traverse to "far, chimeric lands" (from "The Voyage," Baudelaire 1955, p. 137) of symbolic meaning; rather, it is the opening up of imagination through poetic language. Language serves as symbol, words as "correspondences," which connect the two sides of the gap, matter with spirit.

Poetry as an "invitation to the voyage" of language immerses one in language itself. Subjectivity or "life" is lost, and a larger life comes into play. One is imaged by scenes themselves, the subject created into an object. One is lived by words, and words themselves observe the individual. .

> Nature is a temple where living pillars
> Let sometimes emerge confused words:
> Man crosses it through forests of symbols
> Which watch him with intimate eyes.
>
> (from "Correspondences," Baudelaire 1947, p. 23)

Language becomes a female body enveloping individual consciousness.

> Naked, then, she was to all of my worship,
> Smiling in triumph from the heights of her couch
> At my desire advancing, as gentle and deep
> As the sea sending its waves to the warm beach.
>
> (from "Jewels," Baudelaire 1955, p. 23)

Poetic language is itself the place where signifying sign and signified meaning come together.

To see poetically is to approach the world without intent
or preconception, and then the goal becomes multifaceted and
enveloping.

> But the true travellers are those who go
> Only to get away: hearts like balloons
> Unballasted, with their own fate aglow,
> Who know not why they fly with the monsoons . . . .
> Singular game! Where the goal changes places;
> The winning-post is nowhere, yet all around.
>
> (from "The Voyage," Baudelaire 1955, p. 135)

Heroic intention that focuses its eye on the spiritual horizon
only leads, paradoxically, to running aground on materialism or
literalness.

> The fool that dotes on far, chimeric lands—
> Put him in irons or feed him to the shark!
> The drunken sailor's visionary lands
> Can only leave the bitter truth more stark.
>
> (Ibid., p. 137)

The sails of the drunken sailor voyaging by means of language are the stuff of soul—memory, imagination, and dreams—at
the same time themselves the goal.

> How vast the world is by the light of lamps
> But in the eyes of memory how slight!
>
> (from "The Voyage," Baudelaire 1955, p. 133)

Amazing travellers, what noble stories
We read in deep oceans of your gaze
Show us your memory's casket, and the glories
Streaming from gems made out of stars and rays

We, too, would roam without a sail or steam,
And to combat the boredom of our jail
Would stretch like canvas on our souls, a dream,
Framed in horizons, of the seas you sail.

(Ibid., p. 137)

Death is the "old Captain," giving over the ego, giving over control and intention—"Leave all behind" (from "The Voyage," Baudelaire 1955, p. 143). The voyage of imagination bridges the gap between sign and signified, subject and object, mundane and sacred. It is death to the author, the sense of self-certain control of modernist rationalism, opening imaginal vision to life.

O Death, old Captain, it is time. Weigh anchor!
To sail beyond the doldrums of our days.
Though black as pitch the sea and sky, we hanker
For space; you know our hearts are full of rays.

Pour us your poison to revive our soul!
It cheers the burning quest that we pursue,
Careless if Hell or Heaven be our goal,
Beyond the known world to seek out the New!

(Ibid., p. 145)

The dissolution of the ego in delirious voyage is carried further by Arthur Rimbaud in his image of "the drunken boat," where the intoxicated subjectivity of poetic language is bestowed upon the vessel itself. Rimbaud parallels Baudelaire with the idea that since we are being carried by language we are presented with the necessity of giving ourselves up to the voyage of language. It is a journey that is actually not a trip because the "death of the author" means that conscious intention toward meaning is sacrificed. Language itself provides the flow.

As I was going down impassive Rivers,
I no longer felt myself guided by haulers! / . . .

The Rivers let me go where I wanted. / . . .
Into the furious lashing of the tides.

(from "The Drunken Boat," Rimbaud 1966, p. 115)

The drunken expulsion into the tide is an immersion in language: "And from then on I bathed in the Poem of the sea" (Rimbaud 1966, p. 117). Language itself takes on life, each vowel displaying its own particular color (*a*, black; *e*, white; *i*, red; *o*, blue; *u*, green). When language is given its priority and privilege, the inevitable result is shipwreck—"Disaster was my god. I stretched in the mud"—and the subject becomes an unrescued "water-drunk carcass" (from "A Season in Hell," Rimbaud 1966, p. 173). Shipwreck allows for the subjectivity of the world to be revealed where one's existence is founded upon being thought by others. When all reference is dropped, we are left only with elements, no past, no underlying meaning, no origin. Through imagination, the elements of the world become reconstructed so that matter is unified with spirit, "sea mixed / With the sun" (ibid., p. 199).

We are coming to the sense of language itself as world. Consciousness is the pure play of signifiers, and the joke is on the rationalistic mind that suffers under the delusion of control. The poetry of Stéphane Mallarmé takes this idea to its extreme. For Mallarmé, language evokes abyss, words evoke absence (space between words), and consciousness is like a lace curtain blowing in the breeze.

Lace passes into nothingness
With the ultimate Gamble in doubt,
In blasphemy revealing just
Eternal absence of any bed.

This concordant enmity
Of a white garland and the same,
In flight against the pallid glass,
Hovers and does not enshroud.

(from "Lace passes into nothingness," Mallarmé 1982, p. 59)

More concretely, consciousness is like a swan trapped in ice, attempting to fly.

Will new and alive the beautiful today
Shatter with a blow of drunken wing
This hard lake, forgotten, haunted under rime
By the transparent glacier, flights unflown!

(from "Will new and alive the beautiful today,"
Mallarmé 1982, p. 45)

Consciousness as plumage trapped in ice is the poetic imagination striving to cross the gap, thrashing for meaning but necessarily trapped between event and spirit. Meaning lies in the image of striving itself.

Mallarmé uses words with many meanings—a *coupe* is a cup, but also a profile, a section, a trophy, and a cutting—signifiers pointing not toward an ultimate meaning, but toward each other in playful relationship. He takes away syntax, putting words out of order and dropping connecting words, depriving the reader of familiar rational structure from which to derive meaning. Depth emerges in the surface, and we become extensions of language. In the window of reflection and memory, the ego is like a dying man yearning for meaning in experience past.

Tired of the sad hospital and fetid incense
arising like the banal whiteness of veils
To the great bored crucifix on the empty wall,
The crafty dying man his back sets straight,

Then drags along and, less to warm his decay
Than see the sun shine on the stones, will press
His white hair and the bones of his gaunt face
On the windows that a fine clear sunbeam burns.

(from "The Windows," Mallarmé 1982, p. 9)

Consciousness becomes the mirror through which the play of words is effected.

As Harold Bloom has reminded us, the word *meaning* goes back to a root that signifies "opinion" or "intention" and is closely related to the word *moaning* (1979, p. 1). We might say that, for Mallarmé, striving for meaning is a moaning stuckness that can be relieved and loosened up only in play, a throw of the dice. With the illusion of linearity dropped, many presences can come as

DICE THROWN

NEVER

WHEN EVEN INDEED CAST IN CIRCUMSTANCES

OF ETERNITY

FROM THE DEPTH OF A SHIPWRECK

109

BE
    that

           the Abyss

blanched
    slackwater
        raging

                      slanted
               glides despairingly even
                         some wing

                       its own

                             be-

(from "Dice Thrown Never Will Annul Chance," Mallarmé 1982, pp. 107–110)

Consciousness is played by language. We are thrown by language like dice in a game played in an abyss. The abyss is reflected in the space between words, in the darkness of print, in a kind of necessary randomness. All referents are directed to each other. When we go with the throw, there are no signifieds; meaning is evoked in the multiplicity of associations evoked by the words themselves in juxtaposition to the absence evoked in spaces between words.

Derrida and Deconstruction

The thinking of French philosopher Jacques Derrida echoes the French symbolist poets a hundred years later. Derrida considers the ontological foundation of the Western world to be nostalgia. Western man yearns for secure being, a sense of self or presence that he bases on alignment with a transcendent authority. This authority inhabits a place of origin within a hierarchical structure and is seen as inner, source, center, cause, essence, *logos*, the Word, god, meaning, etc.

Derrida sees our very language structure as reflecting this form of metaphysics. We use language to give ourselves a privileged place of presence by assuming alignment with a transcendent meaning behind words or even behind relationships of words. We assume that meaning is present to the speaker simply from the action of voice. Voice itself brings an implication of truth.

In other words, we delude ourselves into thinking we know what we are talking about. Derrida asserts that behind the speech we use is another text. We don't speak, we are spoken. This larger hidden or invisible text he refers to as "writing." Writing is the name of what is unnamed or absent or hidden.

What are available or visible are what Derrida refers to as traces (alluding to tracks, fragments, temporary), analogous to what Baudelaire calls symbols. These are indications of difference and deferral that together he terms *differance*. *Differance* is the abyss, the gap between the meaning intended and what is actually revealed by the words. Deferral refers to the constant displacement of meaning that occurs with language. We can never really grasp meaning or rest on solid ground of meaning because something else—a radical other or absent presence, an encompassing text—is always revealing itself within our voice.

For Derrida, then, we don't write, we are written, just as for Mallarmé, being is "thrown." I would suggest that, from Derrida's perspective, rather than referring to a transcendent meaning, speech reveals metaphors that are themselves dominants or authorities. We live in metaphor. Metaphors don't point to truths, they point to each other. This referral of metaphors to each other is a form of free play of signifiers, much like Rimbaud's drunken voyage. In Derrida's universe, meaning is endlessly displaced from one metaphor to another.

As we are always questing (questioning?) toward a place of self-assured certitude, our text is always revealing the seeds of our own destruction, the disappearance of our origin. The fact is, we are always in interval, always in the gap, bounced back and forth between the experience of event itself and the structure of our perceiving, between happening and creating, subject and object. The traces with which we are left are fleeting, like the symbolist ornament, and less comforting than the palace of presence we presume. We are left undefended by grammatical or metaphysical structure and pummeled by the interaction between intended and encompassing text.

Psychoanalysis

"I look for the forms
things want to come as"

—Ammons, "Poetics"

The thinking of the founders of the contemporary psychoanalytic world, Freud and Jung, is itself deconstruction. The idea of the unconscious is the "radical Other" or the "text" of Derrida. Freud's slips of the tongue and Jung's use of aberrant word associations to determine complexes are like traces, the anomalies that indicate the presence of an absence in language. The psyche's use of symptom or symbol is the deferral and the difference, the *differance* of Derrida. The letting go or voyage into the chaos of the abyss is like the technique of free association which Freud invented as a means of exploration of the unconscious. Jung's emphasis on unconscious universal structures, archetypes, resembles the symbolist poets' emphasis on the symbolic nature of experience.

From another standpoint, the metapsychological structures of depth psychology would postulate a logocentric source (god) behind experience, namely, the unconscious. From the Freudian view, a latent thought, an id, or an internal object lies behind the ego. From a Jungian standpoint, a shadow, or an anima, or the feminine, or the self lives behind a persona. In the various systems of psychoanalysis, authority comes with a sense of presence associated with allegiance to any of these god-words, signifiers of sources of truth or meaning behind experience. The analyst finds meaning and with meaning comes authority through interpretive action invoking a metapsychological grid or structure.

Freud and Jung relied a great deal on the rationalist mode of thinking, which splits subject and object and in which the analyst is the objective observer of the analysand as subject. This mode of analysis enables the analyst to take on an intrepid identity. For Freud and Jung and their followers, the analytic act is performed by the analyst as objective observer heroically exploring the dark recesses of the patient's unconscious.

The hero invites the fool. As Derrida's work reminds us, and as contemporary practitioners of psychoanalysis indicate, the unconscious of the analyst has as much to do with the analysis as that of the analysand. The other in this sense is not just the unconscious of the patient or even the unconscious of the analyst, but the third world that is created between the two. Exploration of this world requires a kind of reverie, a letting go of structures in the service of imagination, an ability to imagine as Mallarmé that "All thought utters dice thrown," to see the emergence of affects and the images of affects that are induced by the interplay between two personalities. Analysis then becomes not so much a heroic endeavor of making the unconscious conscious, but one of sensing and describing the experience of this interplay in which the analyst is both observer and participant. Interpretation becomes not so much a hermeneutic journey to past origin (Freud) or transcendent meaning (Jung) but the free play of signifiers which Derrida sees as the fundament of being.

Jung has described in very poetic language the discomfort

that this approach can be for the analyst. The analysis becomes like the "drunken boat," a voyage without destination, always in the interval, striving to give direction but at the same time giving over to the flow itself. "The doctor . . . exposes himself to the overpowering contents of the unconscious and hence also to their inductive action . . . . Doctor and patient thus find themselves in a relationship founded on mutual unconsciousness" (Jung 1966a, p. 176). At the same time, the case begins to "fascinate" the doctor and the "patient then means something to him personally" (ibid., pp. 176–77).

The analytic relationship begins to take on the quality of "possession," being caught "in the tentacles of an octopus" as the analyst is exposed to

> the most secret, painful, intense, delicate, shamefaced, timorous, grotesque, unmoral and at the same time the most sacred feeling which go to make up the indescribable and inexplicable wealth of human relationships and give them their compelling power. (Jung 1966a, pp. 179–80)

This abyss or chaos results in the doctor having "as much difficulty in distinguishing between the patient and what has taken possession of him as has the patient himself" (ibid., p. 182). Both are confronted with "the demonic forces lurking in the darkness. The resultant paradoxical blend of positive and negative, of trust and fear, of hope and doubt, of attraction and repulsion" is the fertile ground, the analytical third from which a new alignment in the personality is effected (ibid.). Clarity of consciousness is not the predominant quality of experience here; rather, "the situation is enveloped in a kind of fog, and this fully accords with the nature of the unconscious content: it is a 'blacker than black'" (ibid., p. 187). In sum

> the doctor is in much the same position as the alchemist who no longer knew whether he was melting the mysterious amalgam in the crucible or whether he was the salamander glowing in the fire. (Ibid., p. 199)

With the distinction between doctor and patient in a permeable state, the elusive, deceptive, ever-changing content that possesses the patient like a demon now flits about from patient to doctor and, as the *third party* in the alliance, continues its game, sometimes impish and teasing sometimes really diabolical. (Ibid., p. 188, italics added)

Finally, for Jung, the attainment of the goal paradoxically entails a fall. *"The experience of the self is always a defeat for the ego"* (Jung 1963, p. 546). This fall from heroic light results in new discovery.

The difficulties of our psychotherapeutic work teach us to take truth, goodness, and beauty where we find them. They are not always found where we look for them: often they are hidden in the dirt or in the keeping of the dragon. "In stercore invenitur" (it is found in filth) runs an alchemical dictum. (Jung 1966a, p. 189)

The Marx Brothers: Return of the Tragic Fool

The mercurial quality of language which deconstruction posits as the foundation of being is enacted by the Marx brothers in the movie, *Horse Feathers* (Anobile 1971). Groucho is "Wagstaff," the new president of Huxley College. Zeppo is his son Frank, who suggests that he visit the local speakeasy to hire football players for the school team.

> W: Are you suggesting that I, the president of Huxley College, go into a speakeasy without even giving me the address?

So Wagstaff goes to the speakeasy, but in order to get into the establishment, he has to get past Chico playing the bouncer, Baravelli.

> B: Who are you?
> W: I'm fine, thanks. Who are you?
> B: I'm fine, too, but you can't come in unless you give the password.

This is the modernist dilemma—striving to get across the threshold into the place of "easy speak" where word and signified meaning

are united. In order to get there, the proper signifier (password) is
needed.

> W: Well, what is the password?

Groucho tries to bypass the threshold or interval of hierarchical
structure (signifier to signified) and make the mountain come to
Mohammed by requesting the immediate presence of meaning.

> B: Oh, no, you gotta tell me. Hey, I tell you what I do. I give
> you three guesses. It's the name of a fish.

Chico sends Groucho fishing. This is the traditional view of
the work of analysis, drawing the contents of the sea of unconsciousness to the light of reason.

> W: Is it Mary?
> B: (Laughs) 'At's no fish.
> W: She isn't? Well, she drinks like one. Let me see, is it stur-
> geon?
> B: Hey, you crazy? Sturgeon's a doctor cuts you open when
> you're sick.

Both Groucho and Chico have turned the tables on the metaphysical structure of sign pointing to signified. Here, the simile and pun
show us the relativity of meaning.

> B: Now I give you one more chance.
> W: I got it! Haddock.
> B: 'At's funny. I gotta haddock, too.
> W: What do you take for a haddock?
> B: Well, sometimes I take-a aspirin, sometimes I take a
> calomel.
> W: Say, I'd walk a mile for a calomel.
> B: You mean a chocolate calomel? I like that, too, but you no
> guess it.

Groucho and Chico temporarily leave the heroic quest for significa-
tion and let themselves go into free association or voyage or
drunken boat or roll of the dice or the infinite play of signifiers,
words not pointing to meaning but to each other.

> B: Hey, what's-a matter? You no understand English? You
> can't come in here unless you say swordfish. Now I give you one
> more guess.
> W: Swordfish, swordfish. I think I got it. Is it swordfish?

Chico breaks the structure of quest, and the signified is revealed as
if present all along.

Wagstaff and Barovelli then switch places, again turning the
tables on the hierarchical structure. Signified has equal privilege as
signifier.

> W: What do you want?
> B: I wanna come in.
> W: What's the password?
> B: Aw, you no fool me! Heh! Swordfish!
> W: No, I got tired of that. I changed it.
> B: Well, what is the password now?
> W: Say, I forgot it. I'd better come outside with you.

Both are now on the outside. There is no signified, only the presence of an absence. In the same way, there is no privilege between
therapist and patient; both are always permeated with unconsciousness. What is available is dialogue—and something else . . . Harpo,
the man without words appears. He pulls out a fish with a sword in
it. Signifier and signified are identical in image, the domed world of
the word, image and meaning, one.

The movement of analytical psychology into uncertainty has
been preceded in many areas of thought and science in this century. Phenomenology, the uncertainty principle, and quantum theory have all revealed the coconstituted ground of human
enterprise. Michael Polanyi (1958) has shown how all science is
founded in the personal humanity of scientists. Chaos theory has
shown that when extreme amounts of data are considered, nature
becomes a roll of the dice with its own order.

Freud entitled his write-up of his case of Dora a "Fragment
of an Analysis of a Case of Hysteria" and thought the analysis a failure because it was broken off by the patient. What we are seeing is
that analysis inevitably is fragmentary and failed. Patients come into
therapy as objects of failed understanding, heavy under the influence of feelings of failure. Therapists and analysts take up their

occupation to contain the underlying woundedness and failure in their own lives. Failure meets failure. Interventions fall flat and silences break rapport. Patients take flight or analysis becomes interminable. The entire enterprise—in its concerns, its focus, its contents, its structures, its outcomes—seems to be as James Hillman (1974) has written, the place of archetypal failure.

In psychology, patients who consistently put the therapist in the position of doing nothing right, in the place of perpetual errancy no matter what is said or unsaid, are called "borderline." Perhaps these patients are telling us that all therapy is borderline, that all therapy is in the gap between science and religion, professional and personal, transference and countertransference, consciousness and unconsciousness, subjectivity and objectivity, inner and outer, intention and event, creation and happening. Therapy may be an impossible enterprise, between tragedy and folly, but it may be only in that interval of space that healing can occur. It may be only from the foggy deck of the drunken boat, having cast off all moorings, that we can begin to see. Emily Dickinson:

> Not Revelation—'tis—that waits,
> But our unfurnished eyes.

>   (1960, p. 339)

6

PSYCHE RE-MEMBERED

DARKENING THE VISION OF JUNG

Prelude: Sons Carrying Fathers

As I reflect upon the idea of memory, I am interrupted by a call from my son. He is using a cell phone to call me from the top of a mountain in Colorado he has just climbed, his first. I remember back, forty years to the month, when I had climbed my first mountain in Colorado. I was twelve and with my father, climbing a 14,000-foot peak. I remember that during the last very steep part of the climb I was above him, feeling a burst of new energy as if the top was pulling me up. I also had the distinct feeling of pulling him up after me.

My son is climbing this mountain with his friends as part of his permanent departure from home to attend art school. Throughout his upbringing, he had made it a special project to separate himself from his father. As a young child, when he hadn't particularly liked the Christmas tree that Dad had selected, he left a notice tacked to the mantlepiece for Santa and everybody to note that he was not in any way associated with this tree.

He had also made it a point to be sure that Dad knew of his disapproval of Dad's packing abilities on all our trips. Now for this, his first big trip on his own, he handled all of the packing himself. (Of course, from time to time he called Dad at the office for advice, at the same time letting Dad know how completely worthless this advice really was.) By the time the car was finished, it was bulging at the brim—the rooftop carrier overloaded and held in place with

*tape, the inside bursting with every conceivable item one would and
would not need in college. He stood back and, surveying the specta-
cle he had created, exclaimed, "This is pure Ron!" And then, for emphasis, he slammed the hatchback down only to have a protruding
object pop the entire back window into his arms.*

*His comment revealed an awareness, at some level, of some-
thing it took me twenty years of analysis to realize: all of us who are
sons, like Aeneas, will always be carrying our fathers to the new
land.*

The Wells of Memory and Forgetfulness

In re-membering psyche, we remember Jung. The contribution of
both Freud and Jung to the modern world, after all, was the remembrance of memory itself, as bodily and mythical being respectively, *and* of the importance of forgetting as a necessary correlate
to memory. It is also important because, in a sense, Jung presents a
problem for Jungian psychology. When an entire psychology is
named after one man, a reality fantasy or a monotheistic fallacy is
evoked in reference to authority—this, not that, is Jung! But there is
no one authoritative Jung; rather, as we saw in chapter 1, many
Jungs are scattered throughout his work—many different perspectives, paradigms, and orientations—and each Jung provides a different way of understanding. So we need to re-member Jung again
and again as a way of re-membering the multiplicity of psychological life.

For the Greeks, memory was a divinity, a Titan, Mnemosyne, a consort of Zeus and mother of the nine Muses. Archetyp-
ally, memory is associated with wellsprings (Dunne 1988), and in
the Platonic tradition, the soul acted as a kind of urn that, if well-
crafted, would hold the waters of memory, and if not, would act
like a sieve out of which memory would drain away (Plato, *Gorgias*, 493b). The "dry soul" was what the alchemists and Jung
would call the *vas ben* or well-sealed container. The unfulfilled soul
is simply all wet and doesn't hold water.

The Platonic soul entering the material world either crossed
or drank from Lethe, the river of forgetfulness. The desire for life
leads the thirsty soul to the waters of death or forgetfulness. The
Greek meaning of the word *forget* is "to be hidden" or "to hide

oneself," often in the fields or house of Lethe. So to forget is to disappear, but according to the classicist Karl Kerenyi, the waters of Lethe arise paradoxically in the realm of Mnemosyne! Remembering and forgetting occur together between Mnemosyne and her counterpart, Lesmosyne. "It is only both the elements—giving illumination and letting disappear, Mnemosyne and her counterpole, Lesmosyne—that make up the entire being of the Goddess" (Kerenyi 1977, p. 130). The illumination of each new perspective of consciousness brings with it a shadow of something unseen. Light and dark go together. Memory and forgetfulness are in a constant rhythmic flow of upwelling and draining off. Two possibilities thus emerge in tandem—an upward movement toward the divine through memory and the downward flow of the waters of Lethe— and they require each other.

Here, another image of memory from Norse mythology presents itself. Carrin Dunne (1988) has had a number of insights into memory using Norse mythology. The root of the word *memory*, *(s)mer* means "to mourn," so already we have a sense of memory darkening our vision and pulling us down in a folding backward, "thickening" movement. *(S)mer* also means "pith" or "marrow"; what we are mourning is an essence. The verb form of *(s)mer* means "to smear" like the application of salve, so that as well as a wounding quality, there is a soothing quality to memory. Dunne finds a physiological metaphor for memory in the medulla oblongata, the nervous tissue continuous with spinal cord at the base of the brain, which controls breathing and blood circulation. She notes that in many languages the meaning of the word *soul* is "breath" and that the rhythm of the physical act of breathing and pulsation corresponds to the psychological act of remembrance through flowing repetition. When mind follows breath, flow results, which brings an upwelling of memory.

Dunne further traces the roots of the word *memory* to the original sound "mr," which gives rise to three distinct related groups of meaning. The first is the sound "ma," associated universally with sucking the breast of the "mother." The second is "murmur," with its connection to the sound of water. The third is the sound "mu," related to words like *mum, mumble,* and *mutter* and the Greek *muein* meaning "to close the eyes" or "to close the lips," giving rise to our word *myth*—that which *cannot* be spoken.

Memory expresses itself in watery voices that both nurture and withhold.

The Norse image of the tree of life, Yggdrasil, gives another image of the distinct aspects of memory. Yggdrasil was said to have had three roots, each with a well representing a distinct quality, each connected with memory—fate, wisdom, and terror. One root extended into the home of the gods and was associated with the well of Urd, or fate, tended by the three Norns who spin the tapestry of space and time. The second root extended into the land of the giants, and its well, tended by Mimir, who was a giant, dwarf, satyr, or dragon, was said to contain wisdom and knowledge. The third root extended into the land of the dead, which was also the source of all rivers—again, death as the source of life. The well of this root, Hvergelmir, was guarded by a dragon, Dread Biter, who gnawed perpetually at the tree. As the dragon gnawed, however, the Norns made a salve and tended to the tree's wounds, again giving the sense of the wounding and healing of memory.

Dunne associates the perpetual gnawing of the dragon to a central void in the human psyche, the place of no place, "the empty place in the heart" where things are no things—the void that gives rise to the ecstatic experience of universal unity or to absolute terror. We typically employ several means to a-void the void, which psychoanalysis calls "defenses"—avoidance, repression, displacement, denial, idealizing, compensating, etc. The more we try to escape the jaws of the emptiness at the center, the more it has us in its grip. This is the dilemma that memory presents us.

Dunne asserts that the god Odin, the wandering king of the gods and guide of souls, provides a model for "making memory human" through sacrifice. In the first mode of sacrifice, he hangs on the tree of life for nine nights.

> I trow that I hung
> on the windy tree,
> swung there nights all of nine;
> gashed with a blade
> bloodied for Odinn,
> myself and offering to myself
> knotted to that tree
> no man knows
> whither the roots of it run.

None gave me bread
none gave me drink,
down to the depths I peered.

(Dunne 1988, p. 126)

Hung up, Odin gains wisdom, for he has been fixed to the world tree, the paradigm of truth and knowledge. Knowing comes through memory derived from "hanging with it" or "hanging in" or "hanging out."

Odin also gives up an eye for a drink from Mimer's well of knowledge. The loss of an eye, the archetypal giving up of literal day-world vision, is the sacrifice that "darkens" the eye, indicating a willingness to see by night vision, to follow the constantly shifting moonlight. To be fixed to the tree of truth, to follow the dark path bespeaks the embrace of one's fate, one's being, and most importantly, an openness to the world generated by the wells of memory.[1]

Re-membering Jung

In remembering Jung we are helped and hindered right at the start by the fact that he has beat us to the punch—Jung remembered himself. In the last years of his life, with considerable help from a devoted disciple, Aniele Jaffé, Jung wrote his autobiography, *Memories, Dreams, Reflections*. On one hand, it is a highly accessible and illuminating, if not brilliantly written work, the place to start when one is exploring Jung's psychology. On the other hand, it is a self-justifying, idealizing account of Jung's life, establishing an unfortunate model by which many Jungians organize and display their own experience—using one's life to exemplify theory and at the same time using the theory to justify one's life. Jung's life, taken as a romantic model, leads to an overly spiritualized interpretation of his theory, while the theory is used to romanticize his life. In order to see Jung's theory psychologically, we need to "see through" his life to the many different underlying texts.

Jung starts with some early memories.

I am lying in a pram, in the shadow of a tree. It is a fine warm summer day, the sky blue, and golden sunlight darting through

> green leaves. The hood of the pram has been left up. I have just awakened to the glorious beauty of the day, and have a sense of indescribable well-being. I see the sun glittering through the leaves and blossoms of the bushes. Everything is wholly wonderful, colorful and splendid. (Jung 1961, p. 6)

The traditional Jungian understanding is that this is an evocation of the *unus mundus*, the unity of being, or an experience of the *anima mundi*, the life of the world. The account alludes to the phenomenology of the archetypal divine child, symbol of life *in potentia* or to Jung's sense of wholeness as the fundamental human condition toward which all life strives. The problem is that something important is missing—people (Feldman 1992). From a developmental standpoint, when there are no nurturing persons for an infant, the foundation of the infant's being in the world is insecure and unstable. The infant will tend to look to the inanimate world for a nurturing gaze. Lacking the sense of being the "twinkle in the eye" of the mothering person, there occurs what developmentalists call a narcissistic wound, and the infant creates an idealizing defense in which it becomes the center of an ideal universe. If the effects of this wound are not worked through, the individual will conduct his or her life by creating a self that is the center of the universe, with other people serving as its extensions.

> Another memory: I am sitting in our dining room, on the west side of the house, perched in a high chair and spooning up warm milk with bits of broken bread in it. The milk has a pleasant taste and a characteristic smell. This was the first time I became aware of the smell of milk. It was the moment when, so to speak, I became conscious of smelling. (Jung 1961, pp. 6–7)

We want to see this as a description of awareness of bodily being or a first image of the archetypal Great Mother at work. Again, however, an actual person to provide eye contact, to help with spilled milk and dropped pieces of bread, and to whisper and laugh is missing.

In another early memory, an aunt takes the young boy, Jung, outside to see the Alps in the red sunset on the horizon. The next day when other children go on an outing near the mountains, Jung was forbidden from joining because he was too young (too

Jung?), and the Alps became, for him, an "unattainable land of dreams." An idealizing or spiritualizing interpretation of this event would see in it Jung's premonition of the unconscious. A developmental view would see in the desire for the mountains a yearning for the stability of a mothering person, environment, or container.

In fact, Jung's mother provided a great deal of difficulty for him. When he was three, she was hospitalized for depression precipitated by conflicts with his father, and Jung developed a severe skin rash in response, perhaps an expression of his psyche's attempt to contain his emotions (Feldman 1992). She was raised in an atmosphere wherein her father, a twice-married theologian, had visions and communicated with spirits, insisted that a chair be kept for his former wife at the family dinner table and required his daughter, Jung's mother, to keep watch from behind his chair when he was writing sermons to protect him from evil spirits. Jung describes her as having two sides to her personality—one a plain, innocuous woman; the other a "strange and mysterious" woman who evoked frightening presences in her room and severe anxiety in her son. To help him feel secure at night she taught him a prayer that depicted Lord Jesus as a winged being who took children to his breast, but she also asserted that the winged Jesus ate the children to prevent them from being devoured by Satan. As well, Jung's mother confided in him information she would not share with his father, giving him an unrealistic sense of his own importance and responsibility.

In sum, Jung's mother seemed to be physically and emotionally untrustworthy. Jung said that after his mother had been taken to the hospital, "I always felt mistrustful when the word 'love' was spoken. The feeling I associated with 'woman' was for a long time that of innate unreliability" (Jung 1961, p. 8). The family maid gave Jung a more secure sense of being "held."

> I still remember her picking me up and laying my head against her shoulder. She had black hair and an olive complexion, and was quite different from my mother. I can see, even now, her hairline, her throat, with its darkly pigmented skin, and her ear. All this seemed to me very strange and yet strangely familiar. It was as though she belonged not to my family but only to me, as though she were connected in some way with other mysterious things I could not understand. (Ibid.)

What emerges is a split in Jung's psyche in his attitude toward women, reflecting the split in his feelings and attitude toward his mother. On the one hand, he could not trust his mother or even the feeling of love; on the other, he felt her to be mysterious and powerful. Jung felt disparaging, mistrustful, and superior toward women, but at the same time was strongly attracted to and dependent upon them.

Jung interpreted his early experience in terms of his own theoretical constructs—his formulation of the "dark side" of the psyche, his system of typology, his notion of the different aspects of the "feminine principle," the archetypal concepts of "anima" and "the dual mother," and his "resistance to the world" as the introverted call to explore the life of the unconscious. But further, these interpretations can be seen as compensatory idealizations and splits protecting Jung from an unconscious rage against his mother, acted out as a child when he was often sick or injured or was phobic about school and as an adult in his ambivalent behavior toward women.

Jung's relationships with women could be described as manipulative, self-serving, and often abusive. He is thought to have had many mistresses, at least two of whom were his patients and one of whom, to his wife Emma's distress, lived in his household (McLynn 1996). He used Emma's family money both to maintain his own family and for his projects, such as the often romanticized tower he built for himself and where he was often accompanied by his mistress of many years, Toni Wolf. He dealt with Emma's hurt feelings by attempting to analyze her as a means of educating her that he had a right to polygamy, and at one time he referred Emma and Toni to conjoint therapy so that they could work out their problems and leave him alone. His children were said to be frightened of Jung (Stern 1976, Bennet 1986, McLynn 1996), he often isolated himself at home, and he left his family to go on trips to observe natives in foreign lands, which he described as experiences helping him to understand his own construct, "the collective unconscious." A famous comment attributed to Emma and taken as a joke in the Jungian world was that he preferred the collective unconscious to people.

Throughout his life, Jung attracted circles of individual female devotees, each of whom he used for different needs both personal and professional. An early example is Jung's younger cousin, Hélène, who developed a crush on him as a young man. Jung organized a séance group that included his mother and other members of a circle of family and friends, using Hélène as a spiritual medium. Hélène would communicate with various spirits, and Jung later wrote up these sessions as though they were scientific work described by a neutral observer. In the process, he exposed Hélène's emotional life to the public, took a patronizing attitude toward her, and spurned her bids for attention. Jung saw this episode as a precursory experience, which would lead to his theory of the structure of the psyche as made up of complexes that present themselves to consciousness as personalities. What Jung forgot was the highly charged emotional and erotic atmosphere that he, himself, helped to generate with Hélène and in which he could use her to her ultimate detriment (Goodheart 1984).

In 1904, after completing his psychiatric training, Jung started using Freud's psychoanalytic methods in his treatment of Sabina Spielrein, a young Jewess from a wealthy Russian family. The following year she began working for Jung in his hospital laboratory while continuing therapeutic sessions with him. The therapeutic relationship continued while she went through medical school. In his correspondence with Freud in 1906, Jung talked about his unnamed patient's anal eroticism. The following year, Jung again wrote Freud about Sabina without naming her, this time alluding to her erotic transference although not reporting that she was the same patient he had written about the previous year. That same year Jung, who by this time had developed personal feelings for Sabina, used her material in a talk to an international congress, even though, as a colleague, she was bound to gain access to its contents. In the summer of 1908, the emotional involvement of Jung and Spielrein became entangled; each in essence was analyzing the other. Jung was increasingly desperate about the relationship and, after his only son was born, became extremely ambivalent. Only after Emma apparently wrote to Sabina's mother about the relationship, the mother in turn writing to Jung, did he take action, namely by writing the mother and blaming the difficulty on the fact that he wasn't receiving a fee. After several attempts, Jung abruptly cut off the relationship with Sabina in 1909. Hurt, angered, and confused, Sabina wrote to Freud regarding their relationship and eventually forced Jung to write to Freud (and probably her mother) admitting his own improper behavior.

Even considering that Jung was still a comparatively young man and his behavior occurred within the context of the early evolution of a paradigm, Jung had acted in a cowardly, cruel, and self-serving manner toward Sabina. Although he gained both personal and theoretical insight through Sabina, he could not bring himself to acknowledge this or face the split in his psyche that the relationship had revealed.

What Jung wanted with Sabina he achieved in his relationship with Toni Wolf—an arrangement in which Emma served his needs as spouse, mother to his children, and motherly container for himself, while another woman, Toni, simultaneously served him emotionally, sexually, and intellectually. Those loyal to Jung would say that Toni was a healing presence during his emotional breakdown while others say that Jung's involvement with her contributed to her disturbance (Smith 1996). Although both Emma and Toni harbored ambivalent feelings toward each other, Jung, and the tripartite arrangement lasting forty years, each became an analyst, went through great pains to write scholarly work, and served as president of the Psychological Club. Toni was included in much of Jung's family life but ultimately lived her life unmarried, became a heavy drinker and chain smoker, and died lonely and bitter (Stern 1976, McLynn 1996). Jungians have tended to remember Jung's life with Emma and Toni in terms of his theoretical notions of "anima" and the aspects of the "feminine principle" that distinguish different types of women. What is forgotten are the splits in Jung's psyche occurring in his childhood that formed the ground of his typecasting orientation toward women, and the personal pain and lack of fulfillment suffered by some of the important women in his life.

Jung also had considerable problems with his father. He trusted his father and, in *Memories, Dreams, Reflections*, gives an account of his father comforting him as a small child.

> I am restive, feverish, unable to sleep. My father carries me in his arms, paces up and down, singing his old student songs. I particularly remember one I was especially fond of and which always used to soothe me, "Alles schweige, jeder neige." The beginning went something like that. To this day I can remember

my father's voice, singing over me in the stillness of the night. (Jung 1961, p. 8)

Later he slept in the same room as his father, his father gave him Latin lessons, and when he was seven and sick with croup, it was his father who held him while he leaned backward over the bed striving for breath in the "thickened," "unbreathable" atmosphere of the household.

Jung grew to become troubled by his father's powerlessness in his personal life and in his work. He wrote, "Father . . . meant reliability and powerlessness" (Jung 1961, p. 8). At fifteen, after taking first communion, he felt a profound emptiness of experience.

> I was seized with the most vehement pity for my father. All at once I understood the tragedy of his profession and his life. He was struggling with a death whose existence he could not admit. An abyss had opened between him and me, and I saw no possibility of ever bridging it, for it was infinite in extent. (Ibid., p. 55)

At eighteen, Jung attempted to create a link with his father by engaging him in conversations during which he would attempt to convince his father of the possibility of grace through religious experience, but his father inevitably dismissed his thoughts. Jung grew up struggling with and, from a developmental viewpoint, introjecting his father's spiritual despair.

Jung describes his first conscious trauma as a boy seeing a Catholic priest in a black smock who he recognized as a Jesuit coming down the road and, remembering his father's "half-irritated, half-fearful tone" in commenting on Jesuits, thought the man very dangerous and fled. At about the same time, age three to four, he had a dream in which, after discovering an opening in the ground, he followed a stairway down, opened a door, and came upon a richly decorated chamber with a throne on which was a giant phallus with a single eye. He was terrified and then heard his mother's voice call out, "Yes, just look at him. That is the man-eater!" Jung said he was haunted by this dream for years and associated it to his fear of Lord Jesus, the Jesuit priest, and eventually a "subterranean God," all of which he eventually connected with his sense of the dark power of the unconscious. What Jung doesn't talk about is how the experience with the priest might refer to his fear of or for his father or how the dream might refer to his fear of sexuality, his father's sexuality, and/or castration, all of which are themes that were later played out in his love/hate relationship with Freud.

As an adolescent, Jung once found himself struggling for days with a migraine headache that kept building up until he finally had a vision of God on his throne—a giant turd falling from underneath crashing upon the cathedral below. Jung saw this as an experience of the back or dark or "terrible" side of God that his father would never allow himself to have. This sense of the dark god Jung later used as a fundamental metaphor for the power of the unconscious. What is left unsaid is the omnipotent rage at his father that is displayed in the vision and which later was acted out in his relationship with Freud.

Jeffrey Satinover (1985) has written on how Jung chose to understand his experience through a transcendent, archetypal lens in compensation for the more immediate underlying pain that he experienced in his personal life from an abandonment by important figures in his early life. From this standpoint, the notion of a transcendent self is itself an emanation from an idealizing, grandiose defensive structure. From this view also, Jung's ambivalence in relation to Freud can be seen not so much in terms of a theoretical conflict, transcendent vs. personal, but in terms of Jung's simultaneous need to create a powerful and understanding father and his feelings of rage toward this father.[2] Jung's later disparagement of Freudian theory and technique, which could have actually brought him closer to a wholistic image of the psyche, was the result.

Jung's contribution to a theory of the psyche, founded on constructs describing the autonomy of the psyche as evidenced in mythology, religion, literature, philosophy, fairy tales, and alchemy, also can be seen to have protected and isolated him from emotional pain. This pain can be considered as a source for his splitting behavior with women and with Freud and as a core factor in his emotional decompensation after his break with Freud (Winnicott 1964, Goodheart 1984, Satinover 1985, Feldman 1992). Due to his family background in religion, his need to differentiate himself from Freud, the necessity of overcoming the collective rational bias against spirituality, his deep grasp of the mythopoetic tradition, and the need to defend himself from intolerable feeling, Jung deemphasized the instinctual and interpersonal or, psychologically speaking, "material" aspect of psychic reality in deference to the "spiritual." The result was a deemphasis of the details of the personal aspect of psychological life, the life of unconscious feelings and structures that develop from personal experience, especially in regard to interpersonal relations. In sum, Jung's particular remembrance of psyche helped him to forget the ground of psyche, immediate everyday experience as a reflector of childhood experience, and, as we saw in chapters 1 and 3, led to an overly conceptual and spiritual psychology.

Contrary to what it might seem, my purpose here is *not* to take Jung to task on moral grounds, neglectful of cultural context, or to reduce his thought to derivatives of an unfortunate childhood through analytic armchair quarterbacking. As D. W. Winnicott (1964) has implied, Jung heroically did all that he could do in self-recovery from his internal split, albeit through the use of other people and through his thinking. The theory that resulted was a gift to us at the cost of his self-integration. Nor is my intent to advocate the theory and techniques of developmental or object relations psychoanalysis at the expense of orientation toward the archetypal aspect of the psyche. Rather, my goal is to set a foundation for a true unification of developmental and archetypal thinking, not through seeing them as complementary, but through seeing the one *in* the other.

Jung wanted to show that transcendent or spiritual experience, the intentionality of the psyche, along with material life, the causal aspect of the psyche, needs to be given a place in formulating the reality of the psyche. In fact, Jung formulated a theory of the psyche that placed instinct and spirit on the same spectrum (1969b, pp. 3–234). His theory also gave a place for the influence of personal experience and relationships with other people through structures of feeling-toned ideas. He called these structures complexes and originally named his psychology "complex psychology" (ibid., pp. 92–104). Freud had developed the technique of free association, which gave rise to what later psychoanalysts called "regression in the service of the ego" to allow for the exploration of complexes as a *primary* opening to the life of the psyche.

If "like cures like" as the old recipe says, then in our culture, where the divine has found a home in other people (Buber

1970), psychoanalysis as an intensive encounter with an "other" through the analysis of transference/countertransference serves as the place of healing. Clinically speaking, work with complexes through relationship with the analyst allows the individual to come to terms with the details of how he or she unconsciously creates a world, as well as how he or she acts out of a core image or myth as Jung suggested. The experience of the complex can then serve as ground for conscious awareness of archetypal or transcendent reality, rather than for archetypal reality to be defensively formulated in the service of a complex. Working through the experience of complexes in the context of the analytical relationship is ultimately not just reductionistic, but serves as an opening or a revealing of the archetypal dominant in everyday experience.

When Jung split from Freud, he largely abandoned a primary focus on personal and interpersonal psychology and went into a period of severe psychological disturbance from which he emerged carrying a predominantly rational, transcendent theoretical orientation. I would like to suggest that Jung's later focus on alchemy as paradigm for *psychological* life allows for the interpersonal, what I will call the matter, when given priority and treated with an imaginal eye, to make whole Jung's project of remembering the psyche in its totality. But first I would like to make a foray into a contemporary field of science.

Chaos

The field of chaos theory illustrates my contention that the closer the material details of life are investigated, the more the spiritual aspect of life emerges. Traditionally, science has modeled its thought on linear structures based on the abstract symmetry and harmony of classical Euclidean geometry. For example, the bell curve and most statistical analyses are based on the idea that all systems tend toward a medium or norm. The second law of thermodynamics says that the energy in any system will slide toward disorder until an equilibrium is achieved. Jung used this model as a foundation for the structure of psychological life, namely, that psychic energy will always move toward disorder until a harmony is obtained between consciousness and unconsciousness.

With the invention of the computer, mathematicians and scientists have found that this metaphor, based on a bias toward linearity and harmony, does not hold when the complexity of actual behavior is observed in great detail. System after system—weather, cotton prices, heart rhythm, the length of a shoreline, fish and moth populations, the dripping of a faucet, shapes of clouds, stock price data, paths of lightning, the intertwining of blood vessels, cigarette smoke, the eddies of a running brook, a flag waving in the breeze, cars on a freeway—all appear to behave in a manner that results in something like chaos. Periodicity or repeatability holds only to a certain point and then randomness takes over.

A phenomenon cannot be observed unless the observer has a metaphor through which to see it. For years, scientists had learned not to see disorder in actual data but rather to attribute disorder to experimental error so has to adhere to a preconceived system. (Likewise, Jung's symmetrical, conceptual models of the psyche—compensatory function of dreams, union of opposites, masculine and feminine principles, typology—smooth over the rough forms of actual daily experience.) What some mathematicians and scientists have come to see, however, is that their data, although chaotic, does form actual patterns that, although they may never repeat, are stable. The world is chaotic, nondeterministic, but stable in terms of unique patterns. In other words, natural behavior seems to follow *a priori* patterns, what Jung would call archetypal structures. These structures are not linear, nor do they tend toward a norm or median; rather, they form unique shapes. Whereas deterministic science is based on the idea that long-term behavior is stable and predictable, the science of chaos, which takes into account a vast multiplicity of data, finds that small disturbances don't tend to subside in the long run but have massive disrupting consequences that in themselves form a consistent pattern.

Long-term behavior is unpredictable in terms of norms but intends toward unique, stable patterns. These patterns have often been found to form around a central fixed point or "attractor." Jung might call this the intentionality of psychic life toward a center, but here the center is not an abstract metaphysical center of a unified whole; rather, each fragment has its own center. Paradoxically, the more actual data that is generated, the closer one comes, not to what a Jungian might call a materialistic, deterministic interpretation, but to a spiritual interpretation that indicates the teleology or intentionality of psyche.

Another example: we normally tend to think that we can, in theory, measure the surface of a mountain. We think of mountains as cones, and cones can be measured. In fact, the more accurate our measuring device, the more infinite and unmeasurable the mountain becomes as each particular geological detail in the mountain has its own details, which appear with more and more minute observation. Benoit Mendelbrot called this "fractal" geometry, after the Latin word *frangere*, "to break" or "fracture." What Mandelbrot discovered was that fractals are self-similar, that is, each fragment tends to take on the same shape as the larger fragment of which it is a part. In measuring mountains microscopically, each mountain has its own unique pattern that is made of many similar units of that pattern, just as each snowflake has its unique pattern made up of an infinite number of smaller units of the same pattern. The same applies for measuring a bay as part of a coastline, or a single conjunction of blood vessels in the lung as part of a larger network, or swirling dust devils as part of a vast cyclone. Mandelbrot would say that clouds are not spheres, nor mountains cones, nor does lightning travel in a straight line. The actuality of the universe is "rough, not rounded, scabrous, not smooth . . . pitted, pocked, and broken up, twisted, tangled, and intertwined" (Gleick 1987, p. 94).

In other words, chaos theory has moved science into an aesthetic realm, looking at the shapes waiting to be revealed in the data, rather than ascertaining how close the data adheres to a norm. Chaos science has remembered the hidden, universal forms inherent in the actuality of natural life—what alchemists and Jung would call the spirit in the matter.

What Is the Matter?

After his father's death, Jung took his place as the head of the family, moved into his father's room, and started medical school. During his first year, he joined his father's old fraternity, which held talks and mock debates. Jung eventually gave a series of talks to this fraternity regarding science, religion, and metaphysics in which he advocated combining a spiritual and material perspective in formulating meaning. This intellectual thrust eventually led him into the study of alchemy in the latter part of his career. In alchemy, this problem of the integration of perspectives is formulated as the conjunction of matter and spirit.

Psychologically speaking, what do we mean by the terms *matter* and *spirit*? Matter used metaphorically refers not only to the literal, but to anything immediate, what is at hand, the beginning condition—the earthly, bodily, instinctual, gross aspect of any thing or situation. The matter of Jung's childhood would be seen as his mother's emotional and physical abandonment, his father's depression, and Jung's underlying rage, which was acted out as a child in accidents, faints, and illnesses and as an adult in his problematic relations to people. Spirit refers to the larger-than-life dynamic at work that points toward an unseen goal or overarching meaning in any situation. The spiritual response, orientation, or attitude would be represented in Jung's conceptual theoretical formulations.

In his last great work, *Mysterium Coniunctionis*, Jung shows how, from an alchemical point of view, the idea of the union of opposites, *coniunctio*, as psychological change means essentially the ability to perceive as unified what seems separate and opposite. In alchemy, the remembrance of spirit in the matter, what we call change or transformation, comes about by taking what is at hand, the matter or *prima materia*, applying a recipe or series of procedures, and witnessing the revelation of the matter's actual unity with what we had thought of as opposite, the spirit or meaning inherent in the situation. The alchemists had many names for the matter that already contains its spiritual opposite. What Jungians might call "masculine and feminine," they would call "the dry and the moist," "the upper and the lower," "the heavenly and the earthly," "the light and the dark," "the eagle and the toad," "the winged and the wingless," "the pure and the crude," "the king and the queen," "sun and moon," "sulphur and salt," "gold and silver," or "the fire in the water."[3] Another image of the *coniunctio* is paired animals that alternately fight and copulate—the cock and hen, the two serpents of the caduceus, two dragons, the red and the green lion.

The alchemists took as one of their tasks the development of a language or way of seeing that would hold two contradictory elements in a single image or, in Jung's words, the same breath (Jung 1963, p. 42). They strove to remember that within the "visible," the matter at hand, was an "invisible" life or spirit to be revealed. For example, if we think of memory as the container of the "water of life," that is, experience in all of its aspects, then alchemical remembering can be seen in a recipe that describes a king, ready for battle, demanding a drink but being unable to stop drinking until he became engorged with water. We would say that the matter to be worked upon was the king's thirst for experience. The king was placed in a sweat house and, after emerging as though dead, was cut up into a powder, given an application of salve, baked, melted, drained into the appropriate vessel, and finally revived as a renewed personality, an expression of the meaning or goal that was concealed in the old personality (ibid., pp. 266ff).

Another alchemical image for the process of transformation as remembering is *pregnancy* in which what we think of as opposites are revealed as united. In Ripley's "Cantilena," there is a king who does not have a son. The recipe calls for him to return to the mother, and he places himself under her skirts as a form of adoption. The mother, becoming sick, repairs to her chamber and partakes of a pregnancy diet of peacock flesh washed down with the blood of the green lion. Jung interprets the peacock to be an aspect of the queen herself, having to do with containing all of the colors, and the blood of the green lion to be the blood of the king (1963, pp. 285ff). The king is suckling the milk of the mother while the mother drinks the blood of the king—an image in which two aspects we usually think of as separate, masculine and feminine, are connected from the start, each linked to the other in mutual feedback. The king becomes a fetus that eventually dies in utero and putrefies, turning the mother into Luna, goddess of the moon who alternately reflects light and darkens.

There is much inherent in this image that gives us psychological insight into memory. It is one in which something is created, but creativity in this concept does not mean painting or writing or actively imagining or looking for dreams or doing something when one is depressed. Alchemical creativity means allowing the soul to be created—worked upon, cooked, blackened into a "dead head" ("take his brain, powder it with a very strong vinegar . . . until it turns dark," Jung 1963, p. 435), in order to become the container it needs to be.

In gnosticism, the soul trapped in matter hears a "call from

without" or from the heavens from which it came, and it starts on
its journey of return. What is the call to cook? How do we know it
is time? The call is in the matter of everyday irritation and complaint, the "slime of the small world." The king, although he was
born "without corruption," complains that he "cannot generate" and
"has no Issue" due perhaps to "some Defect in the Originall." The
alchemists stress over and over that the work (memory) begins and
ends with a hidden goal that appears as cheap, despised, vile, "the
uncleanness of the world," or "dung in cesspools," which the gnos-
tics call "a Worm and no man, a reproach of men, and despised of
the people" (Jung 1963, p. 123); in short, the "meanest, most con-
temptible and most insignificant thing" (ibid., p. 122). Jung quotes
an alchemical text:

> Take the stone that is black, white, red, and yellow, and is a won-
> derful bird that flies without wings in the blackness of the night
> and the brightness of the day: in the bitterness that is in its throat
> the colouring will be found. (Ibid., p. 192)

The alchemical call to memory is the initial complaint, the
whining cry, the bitter voice that is the ego behind the ideal (ibid.,
p. 256), the gagging in the throat that is trying to ex-press but can't.
This bitterness bespeaks the salty reflection of Luna that needs to
work upon the sulphurous action of the sun of everyday heroic
consciousness. Jung suggests that life secretly wants this bitterness
so that a darkened, lunar, reflective capacity can develop. When
the bitter cry is heard, the multiple colors of the peacock, a new attitude, can emerge.

The cooking or work or opus itself involves a mutual drinking by king and mother of each other that is also a mutual emptying or *kenosis*. We usually think of empty in terms of the need to
be refilled, like a tank of gas. Full and light are superior to empty
and dark. Empty means void and the terror that "full" keeps us
from feeling. However, we have already seen that in the Platonic
world full and empty are reciprocal and from Dunne that the void
is the cosmic and psychological center. Jung quotes St. Ambrose
who sees both the Luna, the moon, and Christ as emptying and fill-
ing in tandem. "He emptied her that he might fill her, as he also
emptied himself that he might fill all things" (Jung 1963, p. 35). The

need for the darkening of Luna is revealed in the alchemical image of the toad placed on the female breast to fill itself, emptying the woman so that she can achieve the condition of darkness of the new moon.

What is the darkened product when psyche is completely baked? It is memory. Jung characterizes the self or the goal as "the same thing at the beginning as at the end, it was always there and yet it appears only at the end" (1963, p. 155). It is the revelation that the opposites have always been together and have only appeared as contradictory when the vision or the container was inadequate. In this sense, Jungians who look to spirit as complement of matter are working in a dualistic way. Spirit doesn't have to be added; it is already there, concealed in everyday matter.

What is the psychological vision? Jung tells us it is the darkened vision of *imaginatio*, not the literalizing vision that the ego wants, not the ethereal, abstracting conceptual vision of spirit that the ego also wants, but the vision of soul that encompasses both matter and spirit with image (1968b, pp. 276ff). It is the darkened lunar vision that has its own logos, its own logic, its own being, its own eros, its own desire. It is the "eye of the mind" that sees through the matter and finds its hidden goal. The goal is the work itself, imagination, as subject and object at once.

Finally, following Plato, memory is the appearance of knowledge, it is the appearance of self-knowledge, not the self-knowledge the ego wants, this is me, but the self-knowledge of the psyche, which the alchemist Dorn described as being that in which the reference is outside of the interior personality.

> No man can truly know himself unless first he see and know . . .
> *what* rather than *who* he is, on whom he depends, and whose he
> is, and to what end he was made and created, and by whom and
> through whom. (Jung 1963, pp. 480–1)

Self-knowledge is paradoxically being known by an other. Jung says, "'Known-ness' is sometimes represented in a way which the subject himself does not know, just as if he were being observed from another planet, now with benevolent and now with sardonic gaze" (ibid., p. 357). The remembrance of psyche comes with the being knowness of self. Wallace Stevens:

I

A. A violent order is disorder; and
B. A great disorder is an order. These
Two things are one.

II

If all the green of spring was blue, and it is;
If the flowers of South Africa were bright
On the tables of Connecticut, and they are;
If Englishmen lived without tea in Ceylon, and they do;
And if it all went on in an orderly way,
And it does; a law of inherent opposites,
Of essential unity, is as pleasant as port,
As pleasant as the brush-strokes of a bough,
An upper, particular bough in, say, Marchand.

III

After all the pretty contrast of life and death
Proves that these opposite things partake of one,
At least that was the theory, when bishops' books
Resolved the world. We cannot go back to that.
The squirming facts exceed the squamous mind,
If one may say so. And yet relation appears,
A small relation expanding like the shade
Of a cloud on sand, a shape on the side of a hill.

IV

A. Well, an old order is a violent one.
This proves nothing. Just one more truth, one more Element in
the immense disorder of truths.
B. It is April as I write. The wind
Is blowing after days of constant rain.
All this, of course, will come to summer soon.
But suppose the disorder of truths should ever come
To an order, most Plantagenet, most fixed . . .
A great disorder is an order. Now, A
And B are not like statuary, posed
For a vista in the Louvre. They are things chalked
On the sidewalk so that the pensive man may see.

V

The pensive man . . . He sees that eagle float
For which the intricate Alps are a single nest.

("Connoisseur of Chaos," Stevens 1947, p. 97–98)

As a boy Jung saw the Alps as the unattainable land of dreams and as a man the unconscious became the great forms on the horizon. What he couldn't remember was that the range of mountains had a mountain and that mountain a canyon, and that canyon a crevasse, and that crevasse a crack, and that crack a nest, and that nest an egg, and that egg a bird, and that bird a beak, and that beak a throat . . . but he did remember that throat had a bitterness. For Jung was the master of dark vision. After all, that pram from which he remembered seeing the world for the first time stood not in the sun, but in the shadows.

7

MINING/FISHING/ANALYSIS

SEDUCTION AS ALCHEMICAL *EXTRACTIO*

As I began to write on the theme of seduction and alchemy, I had also just entered into a classical Freudian analysis on the couch. I made this move for several reasons, one of which was to explore the role of seduction in my life—how I seduce and am seduced. As a Jungian analyst, and perhaps due to the turbulent history of the subject in Jungian circles, I felt a need to extract myself from the Jungian approach in order to get on top of the issue. I soon realized, however, that I had been seduced by something else—the couch itself, which, with its horizontal position, carried me into completely unexpected places. It seems we can never get away from the business of seduction in analysis.

As we talk about seduction, we are seducing and being seduced all the time. How does this work? What is the shadow of morality that exists behind seduction? Why is it that the word is so consistently the object of a pejorative attitude and using the word in this way carries with it an unassailable sense of moral rectitude and authority? Is this moralizing attitude associated with the sexual overtones of the word, and where do they come from? Why is seduction of particular concern in the history of depth psychology?

Historically, seduction is a cornerstone of depth psychology. There was much controversy regarding the seductive effects of techniques that were the precursors of psychotherapy—animal magnetism during the late eighteenth century and hypnosis throughout the nineteenth century. Such controversy resulted in the

formation of ethics committees and commissions which anticipated
current controversies surrounding psychotherapy and seduction. In
1882, Joseph Breuer prematurely terminated his treatment of "Anna
O.," the first case of psychotherapy as "talking cure," fearful of the
seductive influence of the work on both himself and his patient.
Freud based one of his fundamental techniques on seduction, the
analysis of the transference, using the patient's erotic feelings toward the analyst as a means of therapeutic change (Freud 1915).[1]
Jung feared seduction by the voice of a female figure from his unconscious (his patient, Sabina Spielrein) who strongly asserted that
his work was art (Jung 1961, pp. 185–187). In his major work on
transference, he established the process involved in the psychologically erotic coupling between analyst and client as the basis of
therapeutic change (Jung 1966a). In recent years, the seductive actions of Freud and Jung in relation to their patients and even to
their patients' extended families have been discussed in terms of
both the moral issues involved and the bearing they have on the
founding   principles   and   techniques   of   depth   psychology
(Carotenuto 1982, Goodheart 1984, Kerr 1993).[2]

The clinical setting provides an arena for many forms of seduction. Let me count the ways. First, are the sexual seductions toward which we aim our ethical formulations (Schwartz-Salant 1984,
Rutter 1991, Springer 1995). Next are the nonsexual, but equally de-
structive, crossings of therapeutic boundaries that can occur in the
analyst's interaction with clients outside of the therapeutic setting.
Finally, there are the subtle seductions that occur in the everyday
interaction of analyst and patient. Analysts seduce patients with the
words on their shingle: "Psychoanalyst," "Jungian Analyst." Patients
seduce analysts with their sickness, with their intelligence, emotion,
and charisma. Analysts seduce patients with techniques: requests
for dreams and active imaginations, dream interpretations, amplifications, sand trays, pictures, labels, and concepts. Analysts seduce
patients with understanding; patients seduce analysts with the
"search for meaning." Patients seduce analysts with idealizations
and compliance. Analysts seduce patients with interventions or
with silence. Analysts seduce patients with answers; patients seduce
analysts with questions. Patients seduce analysts with confessions
and juicy material. Analysts seduce patients with self-disclosures.
Analysts seduce patients by making trauma literal or metaphorical.

Patients seduce analysts with stoicism and victimization. Patients seduce analysts into terminations either premature or prolonged. Analysts seduce patients into terminations, prolonged or premature.

Any kind of behavior in the clinical setting can take on the quality of seduction. The experience of seduction is of an attraction that catches our fancy, desire, or appetite and leads us away to a place of revealed discomfort, suffering, or loss where we feel tricked and betrayed. In response to our fears of seduction, we strive to distance ourselves—on the high road or the straight road or the long road, all of which carry our comfortable feeling of right-mindedness, innocence, and moral rectitude.

If Jungians tend to be particularly prone to seduction, it is also Jungians who might see through to a deeper sense of seduction. Do not the myths and legends and fairy tales teach us that being enticed away from the path, away from the control of a dominant position, is exactly what is needed for the evolving soul of the protagonist? The mother–daughter configuration is deepened through Persephone's attraction to the narcissus flower, and Little Red Cap is strengthened through being tricked by the wolf. Anchises is horrified to find that he has slept with a goddess, but Aphrodite reveals to him the mysteries of his life. The knight is led off the path by the bounding deer, but that is when adventures start to happen. Shiva is drawn out of his meditation by Shakti, and the universe unfolds.

Here is a personal story. (Is anything more seductive?) I once received a phone call from an old friend from the Southwest, an old dancing, drinking desert rat, a throwback to the beatniks, a former radical environmentalist and a landscape painter in the abstract expressionist school of his teachers, Turner, de Kooning, and Hoffmann. My Dionysian friend, a fellow aging puer, is perpetually wandering, forever looking for that "long lost shaker of salt," incessantly trying to find a place to settle down, always imagining the ideal homestead around the corner or on the horizon—and selling me on it. This time, he was raving about property in southern Arizona, where he already had several artist friends, where Gary Snyder and Lawrence Ferlinghetti were supposedly buying homes, and where there was a gallery with a sympathetic owner in which he could finally have a base from which to sell his paintings. The property, he proclaimed, was near the desert mountains with a beautiful view and a stream running down off the mountains, in short, "ocean front property in Arizona."

Some desire in me always manages to get caught by my friend and his boyish enthusiasm and idealism, his puerile pursuits, his 1950s black-and-white simplicity contrasting with the deep colors and mythical themes of his paintings, his yearning for family and community that seem perpetually elusive, his anger at the Establishment concealing his underlying insecurity, his dedication to his work, his struggles for money, and his passion for the desert, mountains, and sea of the West. He assured me he was getting a great deal but needed somebody to go in with him. I was the first of his friends to whom he was making this offer. How could I possibly refuse?

Caught by the scent of a Kerouac/Cassidy adventure, I said, "Sure, why not?" The next thing I knew, I was headed down the road, my wife and I bickering like Bob Hope and Lucille Ball, to discover my new acquisition. When we got to our destination, I found myself the proud owner of ten acres of tumbleweed in a desert flatland. The "mountain stream" turned out to be a dried-up wash that ran, at best, once every three years. My friend had sabotaged any chance of establishing himself in the community or selling his paintings by indulging in a drunken orgy at the opening of his show, offending friends and potential patrons alike and then taking flight. I was hanging high and dry with my pants down—seduced.

In me, also, something had been exposed, though—led away, extracted, drawn out to drink—something that desired the moisture of feeling for a friend and for creative expression, something that wanted home and community away from the dry, rigid, isolated, saturnine desert into which I had let my psyche settle in everyday urban life.

There are many stories from fields other than depth psychology to show how seduction works in a therapeutic way. Carl Whitaker, a family therapist who based his work on the principle of creativity, always practiced with a co-therapist. One of his images for family therapy came from a group of South Sea island natives who fish for octopus in pairs. A fisherman offers himself as bait and dives down to the bottom of the reef with a rope in tow, becomes entangled with the octopus, and is pulled up by his partner who captures the octopus. Likewise, in family therapy, one therapist gets entangled in the family pathology and becomes "crazy" so that the identified patient can be relieved of this burden. The craziness, now overt and carried by an outsider, can be revealed as a logical part of the family's dynamics and therapized by the co-therapist. Like the South Sea islanders fishing for octopus, tribes in Africa have been known to hunt for alligators by having a man with a rope swim into the river as bait. When the alligator comes in hot pursuit, the man is hauled in by the rope. His comrades ream the alligator with a sharpened log through its open mouth, turn it on its back, and kill it by mauling its soft underbelly. We might say these are both images of what happens in psychotherapy when a complex is teased out into the open through the dynamics of the transference and countertransference. The problem for us as therapists, to paraphrase Jung, is that at times we don't know if we are the bait or the fishermen reeling in the line or the octopus or the alligator.

Power is usually thought of in broad terms of might with associations to Jupiter and his throne or Hercules and his muscle. Seduction gives an indication of the power of Venus as well. Not only can seduction be powerful, but power can be seductive. The seduction of power and the power of seduction can be imaged through alchemy which presents the dynamics of life as a working with metals. Decision making is a function that the alchemists locate in the sphere of Jupiter with tin as its earthly representative. James Hillman has used an alchemical story about the mining of tin that enables us to see more deeply into seduction as a natural process.

> In a place in the Far West where tin is found, there is a spring from which it rises from the earth like water. When the inhabitants of the region see that the tin is about to spread beyond its source, they select a young girl, remarkable for her beauty, and place her entirely nude below the source, in a hollow of the ground, in order that it, the tin, shall be enamored . . . It springs out of the ground at the young girl, seeking to seize her, but she escapes by running rapidly while the young people keep near her, holding axes in their hands. As soon as they see it approach the young girl, they strike and cut the flow of metal and it comes

of itself into the hollow and of itself solidifies and hardens. They
cut it into bars and use it. (Hillman 1975b)

Here we have a sense of the action of seduction serving as a separation of a particular metal from the "confused mass" of the earth
and a sense that its subsequent entrapment or suffering, its harden-
ing and being cut into bars, is what allows for it to be accessed.
What we call seduction, the alchemists called procedure, and Hillman calls strip mining.

In these stories, I am trying to show how the notion of seduction can be seen as furthering psychological processes. Seduction seems to reveal distinct essences in the service of an overall
purpose. The word can be divided into its two Latin components,
se and *duc*, meaning respectively, "away" and "to lead." Seduce
means to lead away, originally from a central or dominating position or system, to draw aside, to lead out of harm's way as well as
to lead astray, to move away or withdraw, to separate off from family or society, to withdraw mentally, to draw apart, to divide or
split, to divert from allegiance.

While the association of seduction with sexual intercourse
actually didn't come about until the sixteenth century in Puritan
England, there is a Venusian element in the etymology of the root
duc that implies connecting, as in duct, viaduct, and conductor.
(Copper, the metal of Venus, is also the metal of conduction.) *Duc*
gives rise also to words like "educe," "induce," "deduce," "reduce,"
all leading somewhere in erotic connection whether out, in, down,
away, or back to the same place.

Seduction, in its original meanings, seems to be Jungian in
more ways than the ones we usually hear about. The fundamental
sense of the word alludes to the same themes as those associated
with the Jungian notion of individuation, a way of moving off the
beaten path, away from the herd, eschewing obedience to a collective or ego-centered standpoint and following a unique, peculiar, or
solitary way. The association of the root *duc* with our word
educate, meaning "to lead out," implies, as Jungian psychology
does, that there is something to be learned from the suffering of
separation.

Alchemy invites us to think further of seduction as a "leading away," in keeping with Jungian thought. One of the identities

of alchemists was that they were workers in metals. Paracelsus defined alchemy simply as the "set purpose, intention and subtle endeavor to transmute the kinds of metals from one to another" (Waite 1976, p. 16). For the alchemists, metals were seeds that had lives of their own, generated under the influence of the planets and other heavenly bodies. Each metal had a corresponding heavenly body, the qualities of which it reflected: quicksilver was an emanation of Mercury; copper, of Venus; iron, Mars; tin, Jupiter; lead, Saturn; silver, the moon; and finally, gold was the manifestation of the sun. The planets were considered to be spirits embodied; the metals were bodies enspirited.

The metals as animate bodies underwent various processes naturally—they lived, thrived, desired, had lovers and enemies, were tortured, killed, resuscitated, and transmuted—all of which corresponded to the various operations in alchemy. Hermes Trismegitus said, "He who perfects these operations creates a new world" (Waite 1976, p. 85). In other words, each metal was a cosmological domain, or a psychological world with a life and personality of its own. The work of alchemy was to help in the transmutation of these worlds.

Each metal had a particular quality of relationship to the other metals. Silver "wants nothing, save a little fixation, color, and weight," while gold "wants nothing." Lead, the metal of Saturn, "is an unclean and imperfect body, engendered of Argent-vive impure (another name for Mercury), not fixed, earthy, drossy, somewhat white outwardly, and red inwardly. . . . It wants purity, fixation, color and firing" (Bacon 1975, p. 3).

Copper, the metal of Venus, is also an "unclean and imperfect body, engendered of Argent-vive, impure, not fixed, earthy, burning, red not clear, and of the like Sulphur. It wants purity, fixation, and weight" (ibid.). Here, the psychological truth of the attraction of depression and passion for each other, which is expressed in Greek mythology in the marriage of Hephaestus and Aphrodite, is depicted in the desire of lead for color and firing and in the desire of copper for weight.

The alchemical idea that metals, as living beings, relate with other metals gives us a psychological language for the dynamics of human relationship. Hillman again points us to an alchemical story, this time from D. H. Lawrence, that helps us understand how our human interactions can most psychologically be depicted through alchemical imagery (Hillman 1982, pp. 133–135).

In his novel, *The Rainbow*, D. H. Lawrence describes the encounter of a young woman, Ursula, who harbors a deep discontentment regarding the pent-up life she leads in rural England, with a young visiting soldier, Skrebensky, and a romantic relationship ensues. Skrebensky leaves but returns a few months later for festivities associated with the late summer harvest.

When he returns, things are different between the two. Skrebensky creates a "deadness" around Ursula that contrasts to the invigoration of the festive surroundings, and she wants to let go, not only of him, but to be gone from the earth. Lawrence writes,

> As the dance surged heavily on, Ursula was aware of some influence looking in upon her . . . . Some powerful glowing sight was looking right into her . . . . She turned and saw a great white moon . . . her breast opened to it . . . . She stood filled with the full moon, offering herself . . . . She wanted the moon to fill in to her, she wanted more, more communion with the moon, consummation. (Lawrence 1976, p. 317)

Here, Lawrence locates Ursula's desire and her sense of imprisonment alchemically in the orbit of the moon. She hasn't had access to moon worship or lunacy; she hasn't been getting enough moonshine.

Lawrence indicates that Skrebensky, the soldier, manifests the world of iron, of Mars. He puts his arm around Ursula, leads her away, and covers her with his cloak. He feels like a "loadstone" to her, taking on a quality of "the dross," "dark, impure magnetism." A "strange rage" fills her, and her hands feel like "blades of destruction." She walks toward the moon, "silver-white herself" (ibid., pp. 317–318).

Lawrence becomes more specific; it is the salt in Ursula that has been imprisoned. As Jung goes to great lengths to tell us in *Mysterium Coniunctionis*, salt, the principle of fixation, is intricately related with the moon, with lunar psychology (1963, pp. 183–192). The couple begins to dance again, and Ursula feels a "fierce, white, cold passion in her heart" (Lawrence 1976, p. 318). The struggle between them intensifies. Skrebensky presses his body on her and wishes to set a bond around her and compel her to his will, but she is "cold and unmoved as a pillar of salt" (ibid.). Ursula's salt is becoming empowered, empowered through its connection with the moon.

> She seemed a beam of gleaming power. She was afraid of what she was. Looking at him, at his shadowy, unreal wavering presence a sudden lust seized her, to lay hold of him and tear him and make him into nothing . . . . And timorously, his hands went over her, over the salt, compact brilliance of her body . . . . If he could but net her brilliant, cold, salt-burning body in the soft iron of his own hands, net her, capture her, hold her down, how madly he would enjoy her . . . . And always she was burning and brilliant and hard as salt, and deadly . . . . Even, in his frenzy he sought for her mouth with his mouth, though it was like putting his face into some awful death . . . . hard and fierce she had fastened upon him, cold as the moon and burning as a fierce salt. Till gradually his warm, soft iron yielded, yielded and she was there fierce, corrosive seething with his destruction, seething like some cruel corrosive salt around the last substance of his being, destroying him, destroying him in the kiss. And her soul crystallized with triumph, and his soul was dissolved with agony and annihilation. So she held him there, the victim, consumed, annihilated. She had triumphed: he was not any more. (Ibid., 319–320)[3]

Through the imagery of alchemy, Lawrence is giving us a more precise psychological language, the seduction of iron by salt, with which we can replace the abstract language of popular psychology ("gender conflict") and Jungian psychology ("masculine," "feminine"). What we call the "victim" is imagined here as iron, and what we call the "perpetrator" is salt. We can well imagine from what Bacon tells us of iron—that it wants fusion and purity—how it would be "led away" from its base or its mass to fuse with salt. Here is an image of the psyche depicted as a matrix of substances that attract and repel, love and war, triumph and lose, live and die.

In alchemical language, the operations featured in what we call seduction are *separatio* and, more particularly, *extractio*. *Extractio*, meaning drawn, pulled, or dragged outside of, is the operation performed by the alchemists wherein each metal is separated from the imperfection of the others. Paracelsus informs us, "By extraction, the pure is separated from the impure, the spirit and the quintessence from their body" (Waite 1976, p. 163). Extraction brings forth essence.

The suffering or sense of being tricked that is innate to the experience of seduction comes from the fact that extraction often is a form of *mortificatio* or death. Paracelsus again tells us that the "transposition of the metals (occurs) from one death to another" (Waite 1976, p. 9). Cinnabar, for example, was mortified mercury while brass was mortified copper. This is like saying that individuation is a series of particular deaths. Whatever the condition of the psyche, it is the death of a previous condition.

Seduction through extraction and mortification is illustrated in the film, *The Crying Game*, depicting a complex matrix of seductions and counterseductions. Jody, a black soldier in the British army in Ireland, is seduced by Jude, a female member of the IRA, and captured. Jody, in turn, seduces one of his Irish captors, Fergus, into various gratifications but is fatally seduced himself into an abortive attempt at escape. Fergus, meanwhile, has been seduced by Jody into taking up a relationship with Jody's girlfriend, Dil, a relationship he maintains even after Dil is ironically revealed to be, in Fergus's words, "something else" from what he had expected.

The core of the film is a parable about a frog who is seduced by a scorpion into taking the scorpion across a river, only to have the scorpion sting him halfway across. As they both sink, the frog cries out, "Why did you sting me, Scorpion, now we will both drown?" The scorpion replies, "I can't help it, it's in my nature." In alchemical language, the film tells us that there are different aspects to our nature that are drawn out of us through seduction. What is specifically revealed in Fergus's nature is not only his ability to be caring in an atmosphere of hostility, but his ability to sacrifice himself in the service of eros for a man, a statement to the contemporary collective that speaks of the love of men for men outside of sexual involvement.

With the alchemical basis of seduction established, we can now gain a further sense of how seduction serves analysis as a fundamental mode by looking at the history of the operation of extraction in depth psychology. In his book, *The Discovery of the Unconscious* (1970), Henri Ellenberger traces the emergence of dynamic psychiatry to the year 1775 and the clash between Johan Joseph Gassner (1727–1779) and Franz Anton Mesmer (1734–1815).

Father Gassner, a country priest, was famous in Europe for his healing powers through the practice of exorcism. Gassner would evoke
the symptoms of a disease in his patient and then extract them
from the patient's body with ritualized declarations.

While Gassner performed his cures in the name of Christian
faith, Mesmer, through the vision of rationalism and science, saw in
them the workings of a physical element. He initiated a new
method of healing called animal magnetism, based on the idea that
a physical magnetic fluid flowed within individuals and throughout
the universe. Disease occurred in individuals through an imbalance
in this fluid. (Jungians will see the similarity to Jung's theory of libido as psychic energy and his notion of the compensatory nature
of the psyche.) Mesmer would correct the imbalance by attaching
magnets to the patient's body. When the patient swallowed a
preparation containing iron (!), he or she would exhibit morbid
symptoms that would subsequently disappear, as if being led away
or seduced by the magnets. Mesmer concluded that the experience
of magnetic streams could not have been elicited by magnets alone
but by an "essentially different agent" produced by fluid accumu-
lated in his own person. Eventually, Mesmer sat with his patients,
pressed the patient's thumbs in his hands, looked fixedly into the
patient's eyes and then touched various symptomatic parts of the
patient's body allowing for the symptoms to disappear. (Here is the
precursor, not only of psychoanalytic catharsis and transference,
but of knee-to-knee Jungian analysis.)[4]

In the history of depth psychology, the chain of healing
procedures transformed from generation to generation while retain-
ing a common element of extraction. Animal magnetism was the
forerunner of hypnosis, wherein the hypnotizer would elicit morbid
symptoms that were then extracted through suggestion. Hypnosis,
in turn, preceded psychoanalysis, in which a transferential neurosis
was elicited in the patient and "projected" out onto the analyst. Jungian analysis made this projection meaningful through the technique of amplification. In the history of psychological healing, from
alchemy through exorcism to animal magnetism, hypnosis, psychoanalysis, and Jungian analysis, there runs a common thread of interaction between doctor and patient. In the language of alchemy,
this interaction is characterized by an aspect of the subject's psychological nature being extracted through a form of seduction on

the part of the alchemist, exorcist, magnetizer, hypnotist, or analyst. We now refer to this interaction in relation to psychotherapy in terms of transference/countertransference, the bipolar field (note the allusion to magnetism), or the wounded healer archetype, all of which are seen as constellated between doctor and patient.

Jung describes the analysis of "every fascination" as a process of multiple extractions.

> We shall, by carefully analyzing every fascination, extract from it a portion of our personality, like a quintessence, and slowly come to recognize that we meet ourselves time and again in a thousand disguises on the path of life. (1966a, p. 318)

We have now come around to the opposite attitude from which we started. The path is now not something to avoid being seduced away from; rather, it consists of reflections upon the various seductions, fascinations, or fallings away that become as the path itself.

Jung describes the attracting nature of the psyche in terms of "fascination," at one time a word used to describe what we now call "psychotherapy" (Ellenberger 1970, p. 151). The *fascinosum* is a favorite concept of Jung's, which he borrowed from Rudolph Otto, who used it to describe the entrancing quality of the "holy" (Otto 1923, pp. 31–40). Jung uses the term to describe the attracting quality of unconscious contents on the conscious mind. The root of the word *fascination* refers to smell, thus the erotic attraction involved in the process of extraction is not necessarily of the genitals but of the nose. Jung describes consciousness as being like dogs "scenting" the unconscious (Jung 1968a, p. 378). Paraphrasing David Miller, we might say that seduction leads us away to an intuitive, bodily, vigorous, earthy, pungently aromatic form of knowing through "nosing," where "the nose knows" or the nose "has to be faced" (Miller 1981, pp. 61–88).

In other words, in clinical practice the therapist will often proceed most therapeutically not when imposing a conceptual model onto the situation but when closely following or "sniffing" actual experience. As we saw in chapter 1, an example of the former would be the use of the notion of projection, an unfortunate metaphor that gives a sense of certainty to the user which is not validated in actual clinical experience. Projection presupposes a

Cartesian mind with a subjective source from which objects are "thrown forth" onto an inanimate world. If I say something is projected, I am positing one living entity—an enclosed soul—but if I say something is extracted through seduction, I am assuming a dual source of energy, that which attracts and also the attracted. Each has a pull on the other.

Jung stated that a projection has a "hook." To complete the image we might say that hooks hold living bait as attraction and are attached to lines held by living entities who reel them in. With extraction, the emphasis is not on the "throwing forth" or "taking back" of projections but on the *reciprocal* flow of attracting and attracted, where the establishment of a logocentric base or source is not only impossible but irrelevant. In 1934, Jung made this startling statement (anticipating object relations theory):

> The word "projection" is not really appropriate, for nothing has been cut out of the psyche, rather, the psyche has attained its present complexity by a series of acts of introjection. (Jung 1968a, p. 25)

The idea of a reciprocal flow of energy has uncomfortable implications for analysts and therapists. Embracing this dynamic, we would be forced to abandon the role of omniscient observer or the repository of projections that are brought to light and taken back by the patient. We would also have to abandon the sense of ourselves as surgeons, the image used by both Freud and Jung to represent delving into the depths of the psychic body. Instead, we would be forced to assume the role of the "hooker," the seducer that attracts concealed elements of psychic life from the patient.

I once analyzed a patient whose fears regarding relationship carried over into the analysis. He was a salesman who historically had been seduced and molested in several ways by his mother. His work and social life were governed by a seductive mode in which he seemed to give others what they wanted while maintaining an underlying control of the relationship. He reported feeling uncomfortable with my silence, said he couldn't read me, and didn't feel I was helping him to set up goals and take specific steps to solve his problems. He felt that I was withholding knowledge from him and suspected that I had a hidden agenda. Quoting from a popular

Jungian book on male psychology, he accused me of being a "black magician" who withheld knowledge for the sake of power. He angrily questioned how I could be a Jungian analyst and not be overtly helping him to solve his problems with archetypal amplifications of the sort offered in this book.

In fact, my patient was right; my silence was seducing him by teasing out his anxiety, which in turn concealed painful, repressed material in various forms. I later lost him to the analysis when I became seduced into a more active and supportive role during a time of great stress. This role duplicated the role his mother had played, which, although gratifying in the immediate situation, brought with it underlying anxiety regarding control and engulfment. Because I had stopped being the hooker and become the mother, it was impossible for him to address this anxiety with me.

In talking about seduction and psychotherapy, I have been using metaphors such as mining by magnetism and the fascination of fishing. I have also used the language of desire with words like *attract* and *arouse, tempt* and *tease.* In doing so, I am trying to bring about a different sense of eros than that governed by the preconceptions of puritanism and which provide the ground of our conventional, pejorative understanding of seduction.

I am also attempting to show that psychological understanding emerges not so much through the classical dynamics of proportion or the mechanical dynamics of rationalism, both of which we are relying on when we use conceptual systems such as typology, the union of opposites, and the compensatory nature of the psyche to explain individuation. Rather, I am suggesting that the understanding that occurs in psychotherapy emerges in the emanations that occur through the dynamics of eros. Different aspects of the soul appear in the world through the movement of different kinds of loves.

We find a tradition for the idea of eros as the mover of soul in Neoplatonism and Hinduism. For Plato, it is the love of beauty that stimulates the growth of the soul's wings and with which the soul flies passionately into the world (*Phaedrus,* 251 a–c). Plato saw all understanding as coming about through the soul's attraction for earthly beauty which starts with the beauty of the body (*Symposium,* 210 a–b). In the Neoplatonic tradition, eros is that which binds the different aspects of the universe imagined as a fountain, animated by a circular flow of love from the source to the various levels of emanation and back again. The source loves its creations and the created long for their origins. Eros, then, is the purposive, the striving, the intending of universal patterns. In this universe, it is the movement engendered by reciprocal seductions that brings about the unfolding of life.

In chapter 2, I made reference to the work of Alphonso Lingis, who asks how a world founded upon a dynamic of eroticism would be experienced:

> Could one then imagine an eroticism that would spread everywhere, invade all the domains of high culture, and not be a contagion of misery, not be driven by frustration? An eroticism that would sensualize the mind in its quest for the truth of the real, that would infect the political order, that would intensify through artifices and in art, and that would be nowhere dissimulated or dissimulating, but discover its climactic intensity in the most sublime forms? (1983, p. 58)

Lingis's poignant answer describes the temple carvings of Khajuraho in India:

> this abstract geometry embraces within itself layer upon layer of friezes where what seems to be a universal combinatorium of carnal positions is brought to the same explicitness and precision. Auto-erotic stimulation, dual and multiple cunnilinctio, penilinctio, copulation, homosexual and bestial intercourse circulate about the temple walls, without primacy of place or of artistry given to any figure . . . . Here one neither descends when one makes love with animals and trees, nor ascends when one makes love with the moon, the rivers, the stars; one travels aimlessly or circularly about a universe eroticized. (Ibid., pp. 59, 62)

Lingis is depicting an eroticized way of seeing and experiencing the world, a vision that is not afraid of seduction but joins with the world in a circular, horizontal fashion that celebrates the primacy of a multiplicity of perspective imagined as thousands of sexual positions.

I would like to conclude by suggesting that if we can make the imaginal leap from seduction as shameful to mutual seduction as a universal dynamic, then our idea of Jung's notion of individuation and the self will change. The neoplatonic circularity of eros is echoed in Jung's use of the term *self* as symbolized in the legendary Echenis fish which

> exercises an attraction on ships that could best be compared with the *influence of a magnet on iron*. The attraction, so the historical tradition says, emanates from the fish and brings the vessel, whether powered by sail or oarsmen, to a standstill. (Jung 1959, p. 154, italics added)

Here the source of the attracting power in the metaphor of fishing is reversed. It is now the fish that draws out the fisherman![5]

Jung goes on to explain that the alchemists sought to replace the fish with an instrument that would produce the same effect. This instrument, the "magnet of the wise," can be taught as a body of practical knowledge, Jung writes, and he makes the connection between this secret knowledge, the "real arcanum of alchemy," and the practice of psychotherapy. The magnet is depicted figuratively in an alchemical illustration in which a crowned figure is raising a winged, fish-tailed, snake-armed creature out of a lump of earth. The monster is the soul of the matter extracted from its imprisonment (Jung 1963, p. 491; 1968b, p. 421). Jung considers the aspects of our unique being to be pulled together as if by magnetism.

> In the unconscious are hidden those "sparks of light," *scintillae*, the archetypes, from which a higher meaning can be "extracted" ("extraction of the cogitation"). The "magnet" that attracts the hidden thing is the self, or in this case the "theoria" or the symbol representing it, which the adept uses as an instrument. (1963, p. 491)

I would suggest that this sense of the self as the process through which essences are extracted manifests in our daily work of analysis in the little forms or emanations that make their appearance through the interaction between analyst and patient— necessarily seductive because they draw out essences. Here the self becomes not a triumphant goal of higher consciousness; rather, the goal is the work itself, as Paracelsus's definition of alchemy implied, a revealing or evoking of essences through the seductions and attractions spiraling between patient and therapist. The self would be represented not so much as a sparkling diamond, pot of gold, numinous globe, or symmetrical geometric figure, but those odd, waxy, weird aspects of an individual's nature that are led out in the little moments of the analytic hour. Jung wrote:

> The *idiosyncrasy* of an individual is . . . to be understood as . . . a *unique* combination, or gradual differentiation, of functions and faculties which in themselves are universal . . . . Individuation, therefore, can only mean a process of psychological development that fulfills the *individual qualities* given . . . it is a process by which a man becomes the definite *unique* being he in fact is . . . fulfilling the *peculiarity* of his nature. (Jung 1966b, pp. 173–4, italics added)

With a nod to Yeats, the center *is* the rough gyration, the slouching turning and turning of Bethlehem and the beast.

8

THE SUNKEN QUEST/
THE WASTED FISHER/
THE PREGNANT FISH

THE SOUL IN UNCERTAINTY

Death of the Author—A Prelude

When I was in my early twenties, I came to New York to learn how to write plays. Previously, I had been working in Chicago—popping popcorn in the Fiddle Faddle factory. Sweating and sleeveless, I shoveled heaps of corn seed into the gaping maws of revolving ovens churning away over blazing gases, like a Marxist phallic hero laboring at the fiery vulva of a Great Mother goddess or an alchemical priest of Vulcan molding the forms of civilization. But when I pulled the release lever on the oven, I became more like Buster Keaton, mute, engulfed, smothered in avalanches of materialized hot air, cascades of popped corn like ghost poop flowing over me into a trough of sugary caramel syrup where it was molded into globs of junk food. My mind became clogged and heavy, my brain addled, and I developed ear infections.

By the time I arrived in New York, I was ready to ascend to the rarified atmosphere of cultural life. I came up the stairs of my subway station, ripe with anticipation of a new dawning—only to emerge into a deserted street and be greeted by a store window full of packaged Fiddle Faddle.

I don't know if my head had been inundated with too much

hot air or my well had run dry, but I found in the days that followed that I simply could not write. I was void, empty, blank in front of the white page, as though I had stood up to speak and opened my mouth and nothing had come out. Disillusioned, I abandoned the quest to become a writer and turned to a more direct form of personal expression—acting in nude theater.[1] That was the sixties. Thirty years later, I found myself sitting with a new patient, whose problem was that he could not write.

Crisis and Quest

In the last book of the *Republic*, Plato imagines the souls of the dead selecting their next existence. Animals and humans alike clothe themselves in the body they will next inhabit in their earthly life. The last lot falls to Odysseus, and remembering his former toils as the archhero of the journey, he searches until he finally finds the body he is looking for. It is lying in a corner, completely disregarded by the others—the life of an ordinary citizen who forgoes ambition, stays home, and minds his own business.

The formative years of depth psychology, occurring around the turn of the last century, marked the culmination of the modern mind. Systems of mechanics, hydraulics, thermodynamics, energetics, and economics dominated thinking. Appearance was perceived in sequences of development, cause–effect, and origin–derivation. Reality was what could be seen and measured. Spirit, the sole alternative to the rational, was trapped in the tangential realm of spiritualism. Consciousness was dualistic, harbored within an interior personality, and separate from the surrounding world regarded as object for unlimited exploration, appropriation, and consumption.

For those who wrestled with the demons of modernity, life devoid of spirit presented the crisis of the modern world.[2] This crisis in culture helped move the imagination of many individuals, including the founders of depth psychology, into a budding paradigm encompassing several fields that sought to retrieve meaning from materialism (Kuhn 1962). One of the principle images that informed this paradigm was that of "the journey," especially the journey of return—retreating in time and descending in space—to origins. The trope of journey was in service, on the one hand, to the literal and rational through the maturing of linguistics, archaeology, anthropology, and ethnology as relatively new sciences. Investigators in linguistics searched for a universal original language. Initial archaeological excavations were undertaken in Egypt, Crete, Pompeii, and the ancient Sumerian city of Ur.[3] Harrison (1903, 1963), Cornford (1911), and Murray (1963) conducted their landmark ethnological explorations into the myths and rituals of Greek and Mithraic antiquity. Fraser's researches into ancient and contemporary tribal rituals influenced Freud, who likened analysis to archaeology and whose office was filled with primitive artifacts.[4] Likewise, the work of the ethnologists and anthropologists Bastian, Frobenius, Hubert and Mauss, and Levy-Bruhl left its mark on Jung, who at one time wanted to be an archaeologist and who took several trips of anthropological inquiry.[5]

On the other hand, the worlds of art, music, and literature served the journey metaphorically when they were broken open by forms from native and ancient cultures. African art influenced Picasso, Braque, and the Cubists, and Gauguin found inspiration in the South Sea islands. Debussy was moved by the gamelan music of Java, and Stravinsky's *Rite of Spring*, based on ancient fertility rites and utilizing primitive dissonance and asymmetry, caused a riot at its opening in Paris. In literature, where the novels of Jules Verne had already warmed up the nineteenth-century imagination for literal journeys "to the center of the earth" and "around the world in eighty days," Joyce and Yeats made the journey metaphorical by seeing the universal experience of language, myth, symbol, and ritual in modern life. Joyce envisioned the epic of Ulysses in the daily events of modern Dublin, and when Yeats asked, "Who will go drive with Fergus now?" he was depicting modern man in search of soul through the tradition of ancient Celtic culture.[6]

In the founding of depth psychology, Freud not only followed "the royal road" of dream interpretation (1965a, p. 647), he imagined his fundamental technique of free association as a form of train travel, the patient and the analyst together being like fellow passengers watching the scenery go by (1958a, 1958b). The analytic mode became one of narrative, describing a trail of investigation leading to a hidden source. Jung provided a mythical dimension to the image, depicting psychopathology as a "night sea journey" and analysis as the quest of the knight on the "long road" to primordial experience (1968a, p. 6; 1973, p. 140).

The idea of an inherited universal realm of primal existence available for exploration, an idea usually thought of as having been exclusively Jung's, was introduced by Henri Bergson and Stanley Hall. Many early psychoanalysts contributed to the discussion of this notion, including Freud, who wrote:

> Constitutional dispositions are also undoubtedly aftereffects of experiences by ancestors in the past. (1958c, p. 361)

> I believe . . . primal phantasies . . . are a phylogenetic endowment. In them the individual reaches beyond his own experience into primeval experience. (Ibid., p. 371)

In addition to Jung's well-known excavations of this primeval experience, Freud made forays into tribal psychology; Riklin made inroads into fairy tales; Abraham, Rank, and Freud conducted excursions into myth; and Silberer discovered the psychological value of alchemy.[7]

In summary, a radical paradigm, spanning many fields, under the influence of the image of the journey attempted to extend and transcend the limits of rationalism. By way of this paradigm many of the practitioners of depth psychology organized their investigation of personality through the language of archaeological, anthropological, and geological exploration—traversing, enlarging, and appropriating the psyche as primitive culture or terrain, with analytic interpretation as vehicle.

Psychoanalysis and T. S. Eliot: Kinship In-quest

We have been referring to a new paradigm that encompassed many fields including depth psychology, finding transcendent meaning in the service of a dominant trope: the journey. Freud and Jung as poetic psychologists and Eliot as psychological poet could be said to share a kinship in this paradigm and their work reveals many similarities.[8] Following the Platonic and gnostic traditions, each saw the modern crisis as one of forgetfulness and the journey as a return to origins. For Freud and Jung, the forgotten was a wider and deeper consciousness comprised of personal and universal memories, while Eliot reawakened us to the lost voices of past culture and their connection to the dregs and corners of contemporary life. The effect of renewed memory in each case is a revitalized experience of the visible and invisible combined. Freud called this consciousness, Jung called it wholeness, and for Eliot it was a unification of contradictory experiences that define each other: past-present, inner-outer, sacred-profane, personal-universal, desire-death.

For Jung and Eliot, the journey was religious, a linking back of vision, reflecting or "bending back to" the larger, more encompassing agents at work or play in the moment—what Jung called gods (1967, p. 37; 1969a, pp. 158, 161; 1969b, p. 493) and Eliot called dead poets. Gods and poets as memory displayed themselves through images—for Jung, those of dreams, fantasies, religious art, and active imagination; for Eliot, those of everyday life. Jung regarded the purpose of analysis and Eliot the task of poetry to re-mind us of these images as the habitats of spirit.

Return was not simply a visit to the past; rather, it was a quest in search of the past in the present, as well as the present in the past, each transforming the other. Freud and Jung held that we do not carry memories of actual past experience; rather, we create present images of the past, "imagoes" combining objective fact and fantasy (Jung 1966b, p. 186; 1969b, p. 23; 1985, p. 134). For Eliot, poetry is not the expression of individual personality; rather, poetry obliterates individuality through alignment with tradition. Past poetry writes the present; present poetry rewrites the past.

> Not only the best, but the most individual parts of (the poet's) work may be those in which the dead poets, his ancestors, assert their immortality most vigorously . . . . What happens when a new work of art is created is something that happens simultaneously to all the works of art which precede it. (Eliot 1932, pp. 4–5)

Jung took pains to formulate the itinerary of the journey during the years of his movement away from Freud. Borrowing from the Sumerians, Homer, and Frobenius, he characterized the "night sea journey" as psychic energy in the role of heroic seeker "sinking" through conscious mood into a "dark," "inner" world of memory (1956, pp. 292, 408; 1969b, pp. 36–37, 82). The inner world of memory, akin to the bowels of a fish, provided an encounter with a foreign element, dialogue ensued, and out of this confrontation something new and more valuable, a "mystery" or "stock of primordial images," was revealed (Jung 1956, p. 408). Following Bleuler and the psychoanalytic paradigm of the day, Jung called these images "symbols."[9]

The symbol, for Freud and Jung, was representative of a greater, ultimately invisible value, its meaning. The symbol called for an interpretive journey through a hierarchical chain of factors in order to recover its meaning. For Freud, the quest was one of free association, heroically following a trail of associations to a threatening latent thought. In a less linear manner, Jung conceived of the interpretive movement as amplification, a process of gathering likenesses to the symbolic form, first from subjective experience and then from a wider body of memory housed in etymology, mythology, religion, art, and literature (1966b, p. 291). The journey culminated with the hero reemerging into the light of "a newly won attitude" or meaning, establishing the model for developmental and symbolic interpretation as quest and return (Jung 1971, pp. 414–7; 1969b, pp. 72–3).

For Eliot, the quest was the making of poetry—"Let us go then, you and I," on a journey of allusion. Poetry takes us down the garden path, along the river, through the darkened streets, up the stairs, across the seas, stretching through time to personal and universal experience, the "deeper, unnamed feelings which form the substratum of our being" (Eliot 1933, p. 155). The image of "the hollow men" in the poem of that name alludes not only to a condition of spiritual emptiness in modern man, but also to scarecrows, Guy Fawkes (a figure in English folk ritual), European fire festivals, Christ on the cross, and the hung fertility gods of the ancient world.

Although allusion seems like free association and amplification, it is different from symbolic interpretation in that it does not emphasize one aspect of a connection as more valuable because of a greater spiritual content. From the Latin *alludere* meaning "to play with," allusion is a playful dynamic, bringing two aspects of psychologically equivalent value into juxtaposition, thereby creating a new and more encompassing context. When Eliot writes, "But at my back in a cold blast I hear," in the distance are the echoes of Andrew Marvel's seventeenth-century poem, "To his Coy Mistress"—"At my back I always hear / Time's winged chariot hurrying near"—in which the poet is urging his lover to elude time and, for the moment, death by "seizing the day." Eliot, in contrast, startles us with the sounds of death, "The rattle of the bones and chuckle spread from ear to ear," later elaborated into images of contemporary chariots, "the sound of horns and motors, which shall bring / Sweeney to Mrs. Porter in the spring." What has been set up as a classic scene of romance is revealed as a modern scene of death, allusion paradoxically bringing sex and death together as the co-constituents of a single image. The poem becomes a matrix of surface parallels making ironic contrasts and surface contrasts making ironic parallels engendering a new configuration (Brooks 1964, p. 83).

In other words, Freud and Jung, in their early attempts to elaborate symbol formation, separated the forms of everyday experience from those of the greater realm, the unconscious, in a hierarchical model, creating the need for an interpretive quest (for Freud, from manifest to latent meaning; for Jung, from symbol to spiritual meaning). In contrast, Eliot saw everyday life, spirit, and the journey already integrally united as a single wholeness. A clerk climbing the stairs for a lifeless rendezvous with a typist would seem to be an image of the emptiness of modern-day relationship, which might lead a Jungian to prescribe a journey to the inner world before love in the outer world is made possible. In contrast, for Eliot the journey is already underway in the everyday climb which alludes to a sublime climb, Dante's ascension up the mountain of Purgatory to meet his spiritual lover, Beatrice. The seemingly mundane event is already informed by its sacred aspect, while the sacred experience achieves its visibility in its vulgar analogue. For Eliot, what Freud and Jung called conscious or outer life, already carries the meaning that they located in unconscious or inner life. The visible life of experience, the lived world, already reveals meaning in itself. It is meaning that is not heroically grasped or located as the result of a quest of interpretation but rather perceived through encounter with the subjectivity of everyday life as it presents itself (Beehler 1987, p. 29).

Freud, Jung, and Eliot, each in his own way, show us that we are living a linguistic life of movement.[10] While Jung sought meaning in the concept of the union of opposites, Eliot revealed the meaning already at play in the experience of opposites. While

Freud and Jung regarded the work of symbolic interpretation as the vehicle to transcendent meaning, Eliot saw the uncertainty of allusive play as meaning itself. While psychoanalysis attempted to make dream life a reality to everyday consciousness, Eliot awakened us to the reality of everyday life as a dream.

The Waste Land as Analytic Paradigm

Eliot characterized *The Waste Land* as his list of complaints, while others have complained about it as a project of nihilism. I would like to suggest it as a dark joke made up of an intricately related series of pratfalls indicating the connection of love and death. The poem was published in 1922, the same year Joyce published *Ulysses*, formulating the epic in terms of the daily life of modern man, Freud published *Beyond the Pleasure Principle* and *The Ego and the Id*, in which he delineated the instincts of eros and thanatos, and within a few years of Jung's formulations of the night-sea journey as psychological transformation. *The Waste Land* is, in part, based on the preeminent Western story of quest, the Grail legend. In his poem, Eliot takes the quest and turns it back on itself. Narrative, the idiom of quest, is consistently undermined. Context and syntax shift like desert sands so that orientation becomes confused. Comedy and tragedy, vaudeville and epic, are interlaced such that we don't know whether to laugh or cry. Seemingly contradictory zones of past and present, noble and vulgar, interweave. Themes of desire and death, profane and sacred, forgetting and remembering, run into and out of each other. Nourishment comes with being consumed, connection with rupture, creativity with violence.

The poetic action of alternating fragmentation and reconstitution works like the cycles of death and rebirth it describes, on the one hand reflecting a modern condition of anaesthesia, on the other, waking us out of a sleepwalk of assumptions and preconceptions. Freud postulated love and death as two separate instincts, and Jung indicated the experience of death in depression as a movement toward destiny. Eliot's turn was to present death as co-constituent with desire, each permeating the other in a single, paradoxical image.[11] We are never closer to death than when we are in love, and the foundation of eros is abyss. Meaning is not fixed but felt with the awareness of interplay between the two.

Death shows its hand immediately in *The Waste Land* in the form of a cosmic joke from Petronius's *Satyricon*. Apollo had granted a sibyl eternal life, but she forgot to ask for eternal youth and consequently shriveled up to existence inside a bottle. As bodiless life, separated from environment, perpetually and simultaneously yearning and wasting away, she presents an image reflecting the modern condition.

The poem then begins with the well-known punch line, "April is the cruellest month," and proceeds with the joke—the contrast between the pain of newly awakened lust for life, what Jungians would call the movement toward consciousness, and the attraction of the comfort of death, for psychoanalysis the resistance to consciousness.

Personal memory of desire is broken by a violent unearthing of a symbolic world of death—"roots that clutch" in "stony rubbish," heaps of "broken images," a beating sun, no shelter or relief to man or insect, no sound of water from the dry stone (Eliot 1952, p. 38). The psychological landscape is modernity, but we are also taken to another time—that of the Hebrew prophets who can see through the desolation of spirit to the promise in the stone. From a "handful of dust" springs the song of an Irish sailor calling for his maid as in Wagner's version of the romance of Tristan and Isolde—a call that is answered several lines later by an eerie echo, "Oed' und leer das Meer," "the winds of love blow in a desolate and empty sea" (ibid.). Here, life and death are not only interrupting each other but inextricably interweaving through each other.

The memory of a girl just come in from a hyacinth garden, wet with rain and allure, evokes Dante's beatific vision and a sense of death that comes from the sight of God. The lines, "I was neither / Living nor dead, and I knew nothing, / Looking into the heart of light, the silence," describe not only the sight of God and the ecstasy of human love but also the crowds swarming over London Bridge (which will soon be falling down) like the ancient souls in Limbo eventually freed by the descent of a hanging god who then arose (Eliot 1952, p. 38). We are getting the sense that not only do earthly love and the dying gods go hand in hand, but also that divine beauty is intricately connected with earthly desolation. In psychoanalytic terms we would say consciousness and unconsciousness are not separate and opposed, but both subtly and violently interpenetrating each other through a matrix of contrasting allusions.

Not only the content but the form of the poem takes us into the tension of fragmentation and coagulation as a way of being. Eliot's vision denies us the luxury of belief in universal systems of order or developmental causality. No a priori patterns of metapsychological essence can underlie our interpretations because each form signified through allusion refers us back to the signifier. Any central sense of logos, any idea of foundational truth upon which to establish a firm sense of being, is undermined by the perpetually shifting ontological ground of the poem. We cannot assume a developmental sequence such as present caused by past or a symbolic sequence such as rebirth following death because each is co-constituent with the other.

Subject becomes confused with object as pronouns jump ship and consciousness flits back and forth, at times a seemingly objective observer, at times lodged in a distinct third person, and at other times of unknown origin. Voices come and go. Characters appear like ghosts, merge, and separate in altogether different forms. There is no essence, no ultimate self-presence, and no certitude of a privileged point of view that unites opposites, resolves contradictions, sums up pluralities, and harmonizes dissonance. Rather, there is a simultaneous opposition and congruity, consonance and discord, convergence and divergence. For the journeying hero who intends toward a destination of stability and presence provided by symbolic and developmental interpretation, the path is eroded. Quest has led to uncertainty (see Davidson 1985).

As the central voice of authority perpetually dissolves into many voices, many languages, speech is brought into question. Dante's exclamations of the inadequacy of language at the sight of God are echoed in *The Waste Land* by the appearance of the hyacinth girl, "I could not / Speak." Being mute in the face of the sublime is contrasted to violence done to the mouth in the person of Philomela, the mythical heroine raped by her brother-in-law who left her speechless by cutting out her tongue. She subsequently revealed the crime in a weaving and was forced to flee, eventually transforming into a nightingale.

Above the antique mantel was displayed
As though a window gave upon the sylvan scene
The change of Philomel, by the barbarous king
So rudely forced; yet there the nightingale
Filled all the desert with inviolable voice
And still she cried, and still the world pursues,
"Jug Jug" to dirty ears.

(Eliot 1952, p. 40)

The origins of art and beauty seem integrally connected to violent loss (see Riquelme 1991).

The appearance of absence is not a void, and lost speech is not lost voice. Absence opens us up to a multiplicity of appearances unseen and voices unheard. Violence, speechlessness, and creativity all echo off of each other throughout *The Waste Land* in strange sounds percussing through the poem as hollow syllables uttered by "withered stumps of time." "Twit twit twit / Jug jug jug jug jug jug" expresses Philomela's attempts to give voice with the stump of her tongue, as well as alluding to the vulgar words of birds observing intercourse in Renaissance frescoes. "O O O O that Shakespeherian Rag" from the music hall; "Weialala leia / Wallala leialala," the song of the Rhine maidens portending Siegfried's death; "Co rico co rico," the crow of the cock on the morning of Christ's betrayal—all provide a sounding board to the Hindu thunder's "Datta, Dayadhavam, Damyata." Here, the numinous transcendent voice carries authority equivalent to its analog—the echoes of dull, decayed, violated mouths, hollow vessels, empty cisterns, and exhausted wells of daily human experience.

When belief in an Archimedean point of original authority is undermined, identity becomes fluid, and consciousness becomes kaleidoscopic. When center splits asunder, we are opened up to perfection in fragments of experience. When we are left without horizons of symbolic vision, we find ourselves living *within* worlds (Blake's "tents") of understanding. Our universe becomes a cosmic ballpark with image after image sending us back and forth within an animated environment of continuous flux. Without allegiance to a priori dynamics and systems, meaning is released into the play of many possibilities offered by life in metaphor. As Jung helped us to understand, who we are is constantly in question because we are always thinking or doing or feeling something while something else is also being said, done, and felt *through* us by an awareness outside of ourselves. Our experience is mediated through a world of imaginal presences as things and events that become alive themselves, carry emotion themselves, and make themselves heard through us.

Eliot shows us that emotion is not in us but is carried by the external facts of the world. "Under the brown fog of a winter dawn, / A crowd flowed over London Bridge, so many, / I had not thought death had undone so many" (Eliot 1952, p. 39). The crowd is the fog itself become animated body, heavy, sluggish, half-conscious, hearkening historically back to Limbo through Dante. In "The Love Song of J. Alfred Prufrock," the fog-body is a cat: "The yellow fog that rubs its back upon the window-panes / The yellow smoke that rubs its muzzle on the window-panes / Licked its tongue into the corners of the evening" (ibid., p. 4).

Eliot's images of experience are a far cry from Freud's analytic model and Jung's typology, *participation mystique*, and projection, but they are not far from the postmodern Jung who paraphrased Kerenyi: "in the symbol, the *world itself* is speaking" (Jung 1968a, p. 173) and who elaborated Dorn's notion of the *unus mundus* (1963, p. 533ff).[12] Jung wrote,

> If this supra-individual psyche exists, everything that is translated into its picture-language would be depersonalized . . . not as my sorrow, but as the sorrow of the world; not a personal isolating pain, but a pain without bitterness that unites all humanity. (1969b, p. 150)

In summary, *The Waste Land* grounds the postmodern sensibilities of psychoanalysis, especially Jung, in three ways: 1) We live *within* awareness perpetually presenting itself and receding. "All knowledge consists of the stuff of the psyche " (Jung 1969b, p. 353). 2) Meaning emerges in tangible form out of the interaction of many awarenesses. Jung gives an example of the interaction of mind and object to create world in the form of the leaf-cutting ant. He said the instinct of the ant cannot function without the condition of the tree, the leaf, cutting, transport, garden of fungi, etc., to give it its ground of being. No single aspect of the gestalt can exist without the total pattern (ibid., p. 201). 3) This meaning is the self-awareness of the daily life of the world. "Transformation into the psychological is a notable advance, *but only if the center experienced proves to be a* spiritus rector *of daily life*" (Jung 1963, p. 544). We find the split between inner and outer congealed, the gap between consciousness and unconsciousness narrowed, and the ego-self axis broken, a long way from the journey.

It's Déjà Vu All Over Again

I will call my patient "M" after the name "Minos," a character from one of M's own short stories with whom he felt very close. In Greek mythology, Minos was the king of Crete who was often cruel, and Dante depicts him as a judge in Hell who assigns lost souls to their places. M was thoughtful, mild-mannered, soft-spoken, widely read, a forty-five-year-old physician. He was depressed as a result of having encountered difficulty producing creative writing (his major interest), his experience of emptiness in relationship with family and friends, and a sense of meaninglessness in his life, which felt devoid of spirit. His depression had lasted throughout his life, at times he had been suicidal, and he had been in treatment three times previously with moderate success.

M's early life had been dominated by violence and loss, deprivation and control, and, most particularly, an atmosphere of derangement and death for which he felt responsible. As an adult, he had strived to master situations through caretaking in his personal and professional lives and by attempting to achieve in several avocations, none of which he had sustained. He secretly yearned for a kind of transcendent condition or spiritual life in which he would achieve "wholeness" through a relationship of idealized merger with another person, "both of us writing the same poem at the same time." He also seemed dreadfully afraid of the loss of control that intimate human connection entails.

I liked M and felt a rapport with him through his dark taste in film, literature, and humor and his interest in writing. His depression and narcissism touched similar core wounds in myself, we held a common distrust of authority, and we shared a complex regarding self-expression. I felt a special need to do well with him.

Analysis took place over the course of four and a half years, most of it at three sessions per week. The result of this treatment could be summarized as the gradual but insistent emergence of death as the metaphor by which he organized his life. This metaphor was grounded in his early life and given archetypal dimensions through his imagination as an adult. Death informed the analysis through the permeation of a continuous resistance, based on feelings of hopelessness, meaninglessness, emptiness, distance, nausea, and barely concealed anger. Hour by hour, he would tearfully struggle, grope, and gag with the question of trust—trust in words to adequately convey his experience and provide connection and trust in my ability to understand him.

The work proceeded in a recurring cycle, taking place over different durations of time—within a session, within a week's sessions, or over several sessions—during which M would struggle from despair to a glimpse of relief in a paradoxical kind of "connection through disconnection" before backing off to a renewed sense that "real connection" was not possible. When he was in despair, all effort was pointless, including that of therapy. On the one hand, therapy was just words that were without purpose because they belied the essential unspeakability of the pain he felt. Dialogue with me was "trivial" or "indulging in self-pity" or insubstantial like "marshmallows" and ultimately pointless because, not sharing his experience, I would never be able to adequately understand or "join with" him. On the other hand, words were also unbearable because they brought with them feelings that seemed too painful and overwhelming for M to experience. At the same time, his despair was fueled by a hidden rage, which, when turned against himself, would "level" his experience and make it into "nothing" while at the same time keeping him untouchable. This rage showed itself in the analysis through the muted but forceful disparagement of my attempts to create rapport or offer my perspective of the situation. These attempts only succeeded in indicating to M how separate we were, how patronizing I was, how little I actually understood about him, how trapped I was in analytic dogma, and how impossible it was for him to connect with me. At the same time, when I was silent, it aroused bitter and resentful feelings of abandonment, and then he would refer to me as a "black hole" and mockingly call to me, "Hello over there! Anybody

home?" (I tend to sit up in my chair when I hear my patients referring to me in the same way my family does at home.)

In this aspect of the analysis, my own tendency toward feelings of inadequacy and depression was readily evoked. These feelings would spill over into the rest of my work as I found myself
secretly consigning my cases into various levels of failure. I would
also feel angry at being castrated, cut down, disparaged, and
pushed away and at being confronted with my own feelings of hate
and impulses toward cannibalistic retaliation and murderous rage.

Early in the work an image emerged that gave expression to
M's deep sense of futility. He imagined an infant ravaged and paralyzed by hunger beside a fire in a bleak, cold setting. On the other
side of the fire was the only other object in sight, a burned, charred
rabbit on a rock. The infant couldn't get to it, and even if it could,
there was nothing there to nourish or satisfy. This image seemed to
hold many of the essential dark elements of M's psychic life as it informed the analytical situation—impotence, emptiness, rage, loneli-
ness. As the analysis went along, it occurred to me that these
feelings seemed to pass back and forth between us, each of us alternately taking the position of either the raging, famished infant or
the burned-out rabbit, in relation (or retaliation) to the other.

In additional reflections, I could imagine our space inhab-
ited by figures from both of our personal backgrounds as well as
their archetypal counterparts. As primitive father-son or mother-son
in relation to each other, we might alternately, overtly or covertly,
devour, attack, withhold, withdraw, abandon, confabulate, or become paralyzed. Either he or I would feel in each other's company
as we felt in the presence of our own fathers or mothers—
ashamed, inept, and fearful of violence or abandonment.

Finally, in a mythical sense, the dynamic between us felt
like the tension between two totem animals. M dreamed at one
point that he was underwater and encountered a monstrous fish
with churning blades in its mouth. My animal had emerged in a
dream I had had years before as an image of my chronic depression, a brontosaurus named "Old Blue."[13] As I experienced session
after session with M, feeling with him the rage, frustration, and
emptiness that he worked so hard to keep in check, it felt like the
monster fish and Old Blue circling and stalking each other over and
over—through, around, and between us. Old Blue would be sliced

up by the blade fish, while the fish would be swallowed up, ignored, or steamrolled by Old Blue.

From another perspective, a patient with this kind of narcissistic disturbance is not unusual, and we went about analysis in familiar ways. As we sifted through historical, developmental experiences in regard to contemporary feelings and relationships, elaborated archetypal dimensions, and explored transferential and countertransferential dynamics—all well known in relation to Freudian theory of secondary narcissistic defenses, Kleinian notions of object integration and preverbal positions, Winnicott's ideas of true and false self, transitional phenomena and therapeutic environment, Kohut's concepts of the grandiose self, archaic and idealized self-objects, and self-evolution in a mirroring context, and Jung's views of the autonomous intentions of the psyche, confronting the unconscious through active imagination, and transformation through alchemical interaction—as we schlepped along on our way through these traditional paradigms, a shift would occur.

The other side of the cycle was a movement into a temporary connection in which we were more like the perpetually wounded fisher king in the company of the speechless fool, again with each of us taking one of the parts in relation to the other. Here, M could experience silence as a soothing holding presence, hear his own insights and my interpretations as helpful in recognizing his own experience, and appreciate the persistent and productive aspect of the work.[14] The connection was paradoxical in that what seemed most helpful and relieving to M was not only the voice given to his despair and emptiness but the fact that our relationship convinced him that no voice could ever be provided that would connect him with humanity. As we worked through the experience of separation, loss, and mourning at many different levels, what came to allow him to feel whole was the experience of rupture, accepting limits gave rise to possibility, the feeling of distance evoked closeness, feeling hate permitted love, accepting emptiness allowed for an experience of completeness, and what convinced him he was alive was his sense of being dead. In short, through paradox, M was able at times to open himself to the immediacy of his experience in the context of relationship.

The last nine months of analysis culminated in the mirror breaking. M, having been touched by a kind of integration, retreated for good and the cycle stopped. He became convinced that although he had accepted some important and frightening personal and archetypal aspects of himself through our work, ultimately it could go no further. He felt he could not trust that I would really see him or share his experience of death and he didn't want to give up his idealistic expectations of merger. For M, the other in his life turned out to be a death head having eyes without pupils, as one of his dreams depicted a woman looking at him, eyes without vision for him. I believe that, at some level, he could not bare to be seen and could not trust in receiving, and I could only speculate that this cycle would repeat itself in his personal and professional life. M finally chose to stay between ideal and abyss, suspended by his own desire.

Toward the end of the third year of analysis, M had a dream in which he acted as the delivering doctor in the birth of a fox-faced boy. Although there are many symbolic amplifications to this image, what seemed most real as our work came to an end was a sense of this boy chuckling. He had us, had us outfoxed in our hopes and expectations.[15]

The case spoke to limits—those of my patient and myself and those of analysis, leaving us both, like Eliot's fisher king, sitting alone upon the shore, "Fishing, with the arid plane behind" (from *The Waste Land*, Eliot 1952, p. 50). On the other hand, those very limits were the outlines of an emergence of a third life, a form that displayed something neither of us intended or wanted, an essential void, distance and darkness, upon which no royal road or developmental bridge or symbolic quest could journey.[16]

The Fish and the Intersubjectival Self

In Texas, "Aggies" are people who are associated with Texas A&M University and the butt of many jokes. One day I was driving in the country and came across a billboard that read, "Bubba's Serious Bar BQ—You Never Sausage Meat." The pun attracted my fancy and, as a lover of barbecue, I pulled in to Bubba's to check it out only to find Bubba had lied, his barbecue was a joke.

While I was there, I overheard a conversation between two Aggies just back from a fishing trip. Apparently, they had started out by deciding not to make this another Aggie venture like the many they had been through before. They were determined not to be the butt of yet another joke and not to go about the trip in the same way they had many times tried to screw in lightbulbs in the past. They had said to each other, "Let's do it right this time; let's change paradigms; let's stop being Aggies!"

Now, in Texas, Aggies are not only the butt of many jokes, they also have most of the money. So the two Aggies had purchased an expensive boat, hired an expert guide, bought the best poles and tackle that money could buy, and set out fishing. However, at the end of the day, they had only one fish to show for their efforts. As they sat in Bubba's that evening, one said to the other, "You know, that fish cost us over $6,000!" To which the other replied, "Really? Boy, I'm sure glad we didn't get any more!"

Jung's idea of the self evolved from several sources, including his own notions of transcendent function and symbol formation. Just as the symbol became the aim of psychic energy once it was released from the tension between opposing poles, so also was the self an overall destination, goal, or life's goal for the journey (Jung 1971, p. 114; 1966b, pp. 173–4, 240). Following the classical model of proportion, Jung referred to this goal as a midpoint or center and to the self in quantitative terms of progression—"widening," "enlarging," and "deepening" the personality (1966b, pp. 137, 177, 178, 273, 276). What had been the night-sea journey became a journey to the center of the earth (Noll 1994, pp. 238–240), to the top of the mountain or a widening of the horizon (Jung 1966b, pp. 137, 222–3). The ontological ground of destination provided the advantage of self-certitude and the security of alignment with a logocentric endpoint (ibid., p. 238).

At the same time as Jung described the self in comforting geometric and geological terms, he also referred to it in the disquieting language of paradox, idiosyncrasy, enigma, peculiarity, otherness of personality, irrationality, and indefinability (1966b, pp. 173, 177, 238, 240). Here, Jung is imagining a psyche in which seemingly incompatible aspects of experience are held together in a perceptible way. Rather than a journey of conquest in which the unconscious is made conscious, or an ego and self opposed on a single axis, conscious and unconscious, ego and self go together, permeating and interpenetrating each other simultaneously. In future years, Jung will emphasize the experience of self as a form of

defeat rather than ascending triumph (1959, p. 25; 1963, p. 546).
His images of self will not emphasize transcendent authority but
rather, as we have seen in chapter 7, paradox, minimalism, con-
creteness, particularity, uniqueness, and individuality (1966b, p.
173; 1963, pp. 544-5; 1976, p. 121). Self here becomes a capacity—
for holding the ambiguity and flux of actual experience, what Jung
called the courage to be oneself" (1969b, 191)—or an occasion—
the gathering of experience and form into a unique, essential
"event" or "world" that can be apprehended or a "place" where
paradox comes together (see Scott 1982).[17]

*A man in his younger thirties, struggling with issues of love
and work, dreams of a pool thought to be without a bottom. The
pool contains fish of many sizes, shapes, and colors and is thought
to be the home of an incredibly large and powerful snakelike fish
called the Boudini fish, which has never been seen, and at deeper
levels an even larger, more powerful fish, also unseen.*

*One day, the dreamer is walking by the pool and notices that
several unattended fishing poles belonging to an acquaintance seem
to have fish on them. He starts to pull on one while calling to a girl
nearby to grab another. Eventually, the two poles merge and a struggle ensues between the dreamer and the fish. The dreamer is dragged
part way into the pool, his feet and legs becoming bait that the fish
has latched onto. Nevertheless, he is excited and thinks that surely
this must be the Boudini fish or even the other unknown larger one.*

*Finally, he struggles out of the water with the fish in tow and
gets it into a pan, anxious to see what it is like. He is surprised to
find two small fish, each very round, flat, and thin, without bones,
colored deep purple, and having an eye on one side only. Suddenly,
they both flop back into the water. Exhausted, the dreamer at this
point doesn't care. They didn't look good for eating and were
strange enough to belong back with the other weird fish. The dream
ends with the dreamer consoling himself, "I wouldn't know what to
do with the fish anyway."*

As we know, a prime example for Jung of the way the self
finds expression was in the image of the fish—symbolic representation of the cold, wet depths of the unconscious come up to consciousness, renewal and rebirth, Christ, god in man, etc. In this
light, the above dream depicts the fish much like Jung's description
of the fish as self symbol (1959, pp. 137–141). It is 1) round, repre-

senting totality; 2) weird, indicating an otherworldly quality; 3) small and yet powerful, referring to a paradoxical nature; 4) threatening to engulf the ego, pointing to the danger of identification; 5) elusive, representing a mercurial mode; and 6) from the depths, revealing its infinite nature. But are we not still describing the fish from the perspective of observer, high and dry, cleaning the fish of *its* perspective and gutting the event of its "totality"?

An alternative to interpretation as symbolic quest would be to deconstruct the night-sea journey to find the perspective of the fish (Flowers 1992). The fish in the story of Jonah, when seen as pregnant, might be equally as central as the seeking hero, gestation equally as rich and important a metaphor as heroic journey. The metaphor of pregnancy, like the life experience of pregnancy, takes us out of ourselves and into the life of an other. Our orientation goes from the self-certain, subjective hero striving to find light to the consciousness of that larger form which is already immersing and enveloping us like the water around the fish.

Jung followed a metaphorical tradition and was gestated, we might say, through the metaphor of pregnancy. In *Theaetetus*, Plato has Socrates, who was the son of a midwife, identify himself as a midwife. He asserts that he cares for the soul in the travail of birth. Søren Kierkegaard, in *Philosophical Fragments*, follows Plato when he maintains that we attain the truth of ourselves through the other who is acting as midwife. Each person serves the emerging truth of another. The teacher is one who serves as the occasion for the truth of others to arise. Jung cited Frobenius depicting the sun god being borne out of the sea as pregnant mother or pregnant fish (1956, p. 209). He described fantasy as the "mother of all possibilities," the symbol as being "pregnant with meaning," psychoanalysis as being the "art of the mid-wife," and the transcendent function as a "living birth" (1971, pp. 52, 474; 1966b, p. 265; 1969b, p. 90). Finally, as we saw in chapter 6, Jung follows alchemical symbolism in presenting the psychic process of change as pregnancy (1963, pp. 58, 177, 175, 283ff, 310, 360).

In pregnancy, the mother "shows," making it a matter of vision. Jung wrote,

> *looking*, psychologically, brings about the activation of the object
> . . . the German (verb) *betrachten*, . . . means also to make

pregnant . . . . So to look or concentrate upon a thing, *betrachten*, gives the quality of being pregnant to the object. And if it is pregnant, then something is due to come out of it; it is alive, it produces, it multiplies. (quoted in Watkins 1984, p. 43)

Jung reports that while he was working on the idea of the *coniunctio* in relation to the self, he had a dream of finding himself in his father's laboratory for studying fish.[18] Extending the metaphor, Jung in his father's fish laboratory was in the belly of the fish. The fish of psychological vision was pregnant with Jung.

Jung said consciousness is "world creating" and that through individuation a world is "gathered," not that we gather but that individuation, the third thing, gathers and makes a world, a way of seeing (1963, p. 110; 1969b, p. 226). Self then becomes the revealing and concealing of imaginal presence giving space its visibility and time its voice. Self becomes a moment of encounter, the self-awareness of a world opening itself as event living us and receding from us at once.[19] We have found with Jung that self has moved from noun to verb, from defining or declaring to gathering and questioning. Am I the fisher reeling in, or reeling about? Baiting, or hooked myself? The fish in labor, or the fetus emerging, or the doctor groping? Am I the infant raging or the rabbit charred? Am I author or rumor?[20] Am I calling on the spirits of Jung and Eliot to drop in on us, or a man on stage dropping names?

ENDNOTES

Chapter One

1. This idea has been taken up by Rupert Sheldrake (1989), who believes that natural phenomena occur, not because they are caused, but because natural forms exist through which phenomena can appear.

Chapter Three

1. According to Marie-Louise von Franz (1970), this resolution of the archetypal roots of language conventions comes through clearly in the style of Jung's German original, a subtlety lost in translation.

2. The phenomenologist that most completely embraces fantasy as the ground of understanding is Gaston Bachelard. Just the images evoked in some of his titles indicate the central place of imagination in his sense of how we understand: *L'air et les Songes* (Air and Dreams: An Essay on the Imagination of Movement, 1943), *La Terre et les Reveries de la Volunte* (Earth and Reveries of Will: An Essay on the Imagination of Power, 1948), *La Terre et les Reveries du Repos* (Earth and Reveries of Repose: An Essay on the Imagination of Repose, 1948), *The Poetics of Space* (1964), *The Psychoanalysis of Fire* (1964), *The Poetics of Reverie: Childhood, Language, and the Cosmos* (1969), *Water and Dreams: An Essay on the Imagination of Water* (1983).

3. A psychoanalyst, enveloped in the fantasy of Oedipus, might see my son's assumption of the role of Ares as a means of gaining the bed of Aphrodite, whereas a systems theory family therapist would see Ares' behavior as an acting out of the conflict between Hephaestus and his wife Aphrodite. Regardless of interpretation, it is the archetype or myth which is the informer.

Chapter Four

1. David Miller (1991) points out that Heraclitus's sense of soul is expressed by Bottom in *A Midsummer Night's Dream* when he exclaims, "Man is but an ass if he go about to expound this dream . . . . The eye of man hath not heard, the ear of man hath not seen, man's hand is not able to taste, his tongue to conceive, nor his heart to report what my dream was . . . . It shall be called Bottom's Dream, because it hath no bottom" (4.1.211–221).

2. Freud echoes this sense of dream as "rebirth"—"Every time we wake in the morning, it is as if we were newly born" (1952, p. 92).

3. Freud's trope is reminiscent of Blake's metaphor of the imagination as a holy smith, forging images of perception.

Chapter Six

1. If we think in terms of cultural psychology, it is worth pondering the quality of our cultural memory in relation to our use of water. As Edward Casey has said, we have not only forgotten what it is to remember and what remembering is, but we have forgotten our own forgetting (1987, p. 2). Instead, we confuse memory with stored facts and locate it in computer chips. At the same time, we are a culture that habitually wastes water. Every time a toilet is flushed, a lawn is watered, or a machine is cooled, many gallons of purified water are wasted. With the Platonic myth of memory as an urn to hold water from the wellsprings of memory in mind, could there be a connection between our inability to remember and to hold water?

2. In this light, it is interesting that in his father's last days of life Jung would carry the weakened dying man around the house, just as his father carried him as a sick boy, and just as he carried Freud in his arms on an occasion when Freud fainted.

3. Nowhere in contemporary Jungian psychology is a concept, not even the concept of the self, more abused than "the feminine" (Samuels 1989). What Jungians have used to characterize the essence of the feminine or the cyclical feeling values, as opposed to the linear power striving of "the masculine," is to alchemy essentially that which is either the matter at hand, the *prima materia*, or that which is "other than," that which is different from the dom-

inant point of view, the moon in relation to the sun, or, in Jung's conception, whatever it is that is unconscious. (See Jung's *Mysterium Coniunctionis* (1963) for a thorough discussion of the diverse concrete images in alchemy of "the feminine" as the "unconscious.") The feminine, as an abstract principle, itself is a product of the patriarchy it is supposed to oppose.

Chapter Seven

1. Kerr (1993, p. 145) shows how Freud's early remarks on the novel *Gradiva* make the devices of seduction equivalent to psychoanalytic technique.

2. See *The Journal of Analytical Psychology* 40/1 (January 1995) for several articles on the nuances of contemporary treatment of trauma as a result of seduction.

3. Lorena Bobbitt, the Virginia woman who rashly took a kitchen knife to her soldier husband's penis in a state of rage, might have grabbed the wrong implement. If we consider that, alchemically, power is in the salt, what she really needed was the salt shaker!

4. Mesmer was also a musician of renown, playing an instrument known as the glass harmonica, and Mozart wrote a concerto for him. The seductive power of the glass harmonica was so great, however, that it had to be banned because it caused musicians and audience alike to go out of their minds, precursor to the acid rock concerts of the 1960s.

5. Just as the fish, paradoxically that which is attracted and attracting, is a symbol of the self, so also is Christ, at once fisherman, fish, and bait, a self symbol. He is "fisher of man," as well as depicted as fishing for Leviathan with the line of David. Alchemically, he *is* the fish (Jung 1959). As well, he can be seen as the bait in his descent into limbo, following his death on the cross, which allows for the release of the righteous souls (Kalsched 1981).

Chapter Eight

1. One of the alchemical images that Jung uses to depict the intersubjectival nature of the analytic situation is entitled "The

Naked Truth," in which the King and Queen are nude (Jung 1966a, pp. 236–7).

2. The other side of this idea is that the spirit of modern life is crisis (see Megill 1985).

3. Sir Flinders Petrie and Sir Arthur Evans led excavating expeditions in Egypt and Crete respectively during the 1890s and early 1900s. Although discovered centuries earlier, the excavation at Pompeii was conducted for the most part from 1910 through 1926. Sir Leonard Wooley began excavations of Ur in 1924.

4. See Kerr, *A Most Dangerous Method* (1993), pp. 360 and 396, for Fraser's influence on Freud's writing of *Totem and Taboo*. Fraser also heavily influenced Jessie Weston's *From Ritual to Romance*, which in turn helped to inspire Eliot's *The Waste Land*. See also Freud, "Constructions in Analysis" (1937).

5. Adolf Bastian, *Ethnische Elementargedanken in der Lehre von Menschen* (1895); Leo Frobenius, *Das Zeitalter der Sonnengotten* (1904); Hubert and Maus, *Melanges d'histoire des Religions* (1909); Levy-Bruhl, *How Natives Think* (1912). Throughout his work, Jung uses archaeological metaphors to organize his thinking regarding analysis. See, for example, his description of a sword in a patient's dream as a weapon "of very ancient heritage of mankind, which lay buried . . . and was brought to light through excavation (analysis)" (1969b, p. 76). Jung's description of his travels can be found in *Memories, Dreams, Reflections* (1961).

6. For a discussion of the interface of Joyce and Jung, see Jean Kimball, *Odyssey of the Psyche: Jungian Patterns in Joyce's Ulysses* (1997).

7. See Jung (1956), Freud (1913), Abraham (1908), Rank (1909), Riklin (1907). Although most biographies of Jung and certainly Jung's autobiography tend to idealize him as a form of prophetic hero stemming the tide of rationalism alone, the fact is that many of the major concepts we think of as Jung's were brought into the dialogue of depth psychology by other analysts and psychologists—the collective unconscious (Freud and others); intrapsychic dialogue, the complex, and psychic energy (Pierre Janet); the bisexual nature of the psyche (from the psychoanalytic paradigm generally); the word association test (Gustav Aschaffenberg); the self (Stanley Hall, William James) to name a few. See Ellenberger (1970), Kerr (1993), and Noll (1994).

8. There are also likenesses in the personal lives of Eliot and Jung—both were widely read, deeply religious in a personal way, knew several languages, had troubled marriages which informed their work, recovered from mental breakdowns with renewed originality and purpose, were accused of anti-Semitism, and engaged in sailing for sport.

9. The symbol was an early solution to a problem with which Jung struggled throughout his career—the idea that there was something of higher value, something of the infinite, unknowable, or invisible that nevertheless could be grasped, known, or seen in experience (see Jung 1969b, p. 75; 1971, pp. 474, 476).

10. Freud, Jung, and Eliot were writing at a time when a revolution was taking place in the field of language. In 1915, Ferdinand de Saussure had developed a theory of the meaning in language as being derived not from a system in which words are signifiers referring to signified meaning but rather from the *structure* of words in relation to each other. Freud, Jung, and Eliot each anticipated Saussure's structuralism in that their work reveals words and word structures to be forms with a life and history of their own. Freud showed the structure of the unconscious in jokes and slips of the tongue. Jung, using the association test and etymological studies, intended to show that words, as carriers of complexes and archetypes, contain worlds of which we are unaware and therefore are religious in the sense that they encompass us. Eliot intended words to carry the history of language through poetry.

Further, Jung defined the symbol by using a linguistic term, *analogy*. The symbol is a "libido analogue" in that it transforms libido from its original inaccessible form into one that is more "effective" as it works in the individual's life (1956, pp. 96, 141; 1969b, pp. 48–49). Early in their relationship, Jung wrote to Freud about "thinking in analogies, which your analytical method trains so well" and went on to describe psychoanalysis as a work requiring the skills of a "poet" (see Kerr 1993, p. 111).

11. Sabina Spielrein was the first in the psychoanalytic circle at that time to write of the interaction of sex and death, but her work has been largely left unrecognized. See chapter 6 for a discussion of her relationship with Jung; see also Kerr (1993).

12. See chapter 3 for my discussion of the integral connection of body/mind/world.

13. In the dream, I was watching a black ghetto community sitting in a cheering section at a school basketball game, led by cheerleaders moving back and forth on their hands, rocking and weaving in rhythm to a chant being sung in celebration of the community animal that lived deep in the ground underneath the ghetto, a brontosaurus named "Old Blue." The chant was for the team but more importantly for the community as a whole because the pervading feeling of religious festivity was in celebration of the idea that none of the community would ever be able to leave the ghetto. This was it, their life; Old Blue was their totem-god, and this was the celebration of these psychological realities.

14. The transformative images that emerged in dreams in relation to this world had to do with eating—moving from a self-gnawing, self-consuming death head, to the incorporation of worms from the entrails of a dead wolf, entrail-shaped pastry with gravy, a squirrel, rat burgers, words on cards, and finally Double Whoppers, in addition to images of oral sex with various hermaphroditic and female figures.

15. For symbolic amplification, one could look at many dog-man myths, especially the Egyptian god of the dead, Anubis. See Herzog (1983), chapter 4, and Budge (1969), chapter 16.

16. Winnicott hypothesizes a core to the true self that cannot communicate with the world of perceived objects so that, in a crucial way, "each individual is an isolate, permanently noncommunicating, permanently unknown, in fact unfound" (Winnicott 1965, p. 185). This would seem to correspond to Jung's sense of the unknowable nature of the self.

17. William Blake called this world "an immortal tent built by the Sons of Los (imagination), / And every space that a man views around his dwelling place, / Standing on his own roof or in his garden . . . / . . . such space is his universe" (Blake 1965, p. 126, plate 128).

18. Jung's examples of the fish in dreams often depict the catching of the fish by the dreamer as if to bolster his argument concerning the notion of the self with a fine catch. In his autobiography, Jung reports that he came to his ideas concerning the symbolism of the fish during a critical period in his thinking about the *coniunctio* (1961, 213–14). He dreamed that he entered a unknown part of his house and found himself in his father's workroom,

which had been turned into a laboratory for the study of fish. In his associations, Jung thought of his father as being like the fisher king, stricken with a wound that would not heal. As a boy, Jung was like Parsifal, without speech, therefore unable to help his father. Jung concluded that his father's sufferings were an imitation of the sufferings of Christ, the fish, and the suffering of the collective Christian. Like Christ, his father became a caretaker of souls (in another dream his father's Bible is bound in fish skin) and his fish laboratory was, itself, the ecclesiastical cure of souls.

19. Blake thought of this as "a Moment in each Day that Satan cannot find, / Nor can his Watch Fiends find it, but the Industrious find / This Moment and it multiply; and when it once is found, / It renovates every Moment of the Day if rightly placed" (Blake 1965, p. 135, plate 35).

20. The artist William de Kooning said that he was the source of a rumor concerning his drawings.

BIBLIOGRAPHY

Abraham, K. 1908. Dreams and myth. In Sigmund Freud, ed., *Schriften zur angewandten Seelenkunde*, no. 4. Leipzig.

Achterberg, J. and F. Lawlis. 1980. *Bridges of the Bodymind*. Champaign, Ill.: Institute for Personality and Ability Testing.

Ammons, A. R. 1972. *Collected Poems 1951–1971*. New York: W. W. Norton.

Anobile, R., ed. 1971. *Why a Duck*. New York: Harper and Row.

Bacon, R. 1975. *The Mirror of Alchemy*. Los Angeles: The Globe Bookstore.

Baudelaire, C. 1947. *The Flowers of Evil*. G. Wagner, trans. Norfolk, Va.: New Directions.

———. 1955. *Flowers of Evil*. M. and J. Mathews, eds. New York: New Directions Press.

Beehler, M. 1987. *T. S. Eliot, Wallace Stevens and the Discourses of Difference*. Baton Rouge, La.: Louisiana State University Press.

Bennet, G. 1986. Domestic life with C. G. Jung. *Spring* 1986:177–189.

Berry, P. 1974. An approach to the dream. *Spring,* 1974:58–79.

———. 1983. Jung's early psychiatric writing: The emergence of a psychopoetics. Ph.D. diss., University of Dallas.

Blake, W. 1965. *The Poetry and Prose of William Blake*. D. Erdman, ed. Garden City, N.Y.: Doubleday.

Bloom, H. 1979. The breaking of form. In Bloom et al., *Deconstruction and Criticism*. New York: Continuum.

Bosnak, R. 1988. *A Little Course in Dreams*. Boston: Shambala.

———. 1996. *Tracks in the Wilderness of Dreaming*. New York: Delta.

Boss, M. 1977. Dreaming and the dreamed in the daseinsanalytical way of seeing. In C. Scott, ed., *On Dreaming: An Encounter with Medard Boss*. Chico, Calif.: Scholars Press.

Brooke, R. 1991. *Jung and Phenomenology*. London: Routledge.

Brooks, C. 1964. The beliefs embodied in the work. In R. Knoll, ed., *Storm Over The Waste Land*. Chicago: Scott Foresman.

Buber, M. 1970. *I and Thou*. W. Kaufmann, trans. New York: Charles Scribner's Sons.

Budge, E. A. Wallace. 1969. *The Gods of the Egyptians*. New York: Dover.

Carotenuto, A. 1982. *A Secret Symmetry*. New York: Pantheon Books.

Casey, E. 1987. *Remembering: A Phenomenological Study*. Bloomington, Ind.: Indiana University Press.

Cornford, F. M. 1911. *The Origins of Attic Comedy*. Garden City, N.Y.: Doubleday.

Crossan, J. D. 1976. *Raid on the Articulate: Cosmic Eschatology in Jesus and Broges*. New York: Harper and Row.

———. 1980. *Cliffs of Fall: Paradox and Parables of Jesus*. New York: The Seabury Press.

Davidson, H. 1985. *T. S. Eliot and Hermeneutics*. Baton Rouge, La.: Louisiana State University Press.

Derrida, J. 1970. Structure, sign, and play in the discourse of the human sciences. In R. Macksey and E. Donato, eds., *The Languages of Criticism and the Sciences of Man: The Structuralist Controversy*. Baltimore: Johns Hopkins Press.

———. 1976. *Of Grammatology*. G. Spivak, trans. Baltimore: John Hopkins University Press.

Dickinson, E. 1960. *The Complete Poems of Emily Dickinson*. Thomas H. Johnson, ed. Boston: Little, Brown and Co.

Dunne, C. 1988. The roots of memory. *Spring*, 1988:113–128.

Eliot, T. S. 1932. Tradition and the individual talent. In *Selected Essays*. New York: Harcourt, Brace, and Company.

———. 1933. *The Use of Poetry and the Use of Criticism*. New York: Barnes and Noble.

———. 1952. *The Complete Poems and Plays 1909–1950*. New York: Harcourt, Brace and World, Inc.

Ellenberger, H. 1970. *The Discovery of the Unconscious*. New York: Basic Books.

Feldman, B. 1992. Jung's infancy and childhood and its influence upon the development of analytical psychology. *Journal of Analytical Psychology* 37:255–274.

Flowers, B. S. 1992. Deconstructing the night sea journey: The whale's perspective. Paper presented at conference, Following the Spirit: Jung and Postmodernism, Dallas.

Freud, S. 1913. *Totem and Taboo*. A. A. Brill, trans. New York: Vintage Books.

———. 1915. Observations on transference-love. *SE*, vol. 12. London: Hogarth Press.

———. 1937. Constructions in analysis. In Phillop Rieff, ed., *Sigmund Freud: Therapy and Technique*. New York: Collier Books, 1963.

———. 1952. *A General Introduction to Psychoanalysis*. J. Riviere, trans. New York: Washington Square Press.

———. 1958a. On beginning the treatment. *SE*, vol. 12. London: Hogarth Press.

———. 1958b. Recommendations to physicians practicing psychoanalysis. *SE*, vol. 12. London: Hogarth Press.

———. 1958c. The paths to the formation of symptoms. *SE*, vol. 16. London: Hogarth Press.

———. 1960. *The Psychopathology of Everyday Life*. trans. A. Tyson, New York: W. W. Norton.

———. 1963. *Dora: An Analysis of a Case of Hysteria*. New York: Collier Books.

———. 1965a. *The Interpretation of Dreams*. J. Strachey, trans. New York: Avon Books.

———. 1965b. *New Introductory Lectures on Psychoanalysis*. J. Strachey, trans. New York: W. W. Norton and Company.

———. 1969. *An Outline of Psycho-analysis*. J. Strachey, trans. New York: W. W. Norton and Company.

Gleick, J. 1987. *Chaos: Making a New Science*. New York: Penguin Books.

Goodheart, W. 1984. C. G. Jung's first 'patient': On the seminal emergence of Jung's thought. *Journal of Analytical Psychology* 29:35–56.

Hadas, M., ed. 1961. *Essential Works of Stoicism*. New York: Bantam Books.

Harrison, J. 1903. *Prolegomena to the Study of Greek Religion*. London: Merlin Press, 1962.

———. 1963. *Themis: A Study of the Social Origins of Greek Religion*. London: Merlin Press.

Heidegger, M. 1962. *Being and Time*. John Macquarrie and Edward Robinson, trans. New York: Harper and Row.

Herzog, Edgar. 1983. *Psyche and Death*. Dallas: Spring.

Hillman, J. 1974. Three ways of failure and analysis. In G. Adler, ed., *Success and Failure in Analysis*. New York: G. P. Putnam's Sons.

———. 1975a. The fiction of case history: A round. In J. B. Wiggins, ed., *Religion as Story*. New York: Harper and Row.

———. 1975b. Unpublished notes from New Mexico Seminar on Alchemy.

———. 1977. An inquiry into image. *Spring*, 1977:62–88.

———. 1978. Further notes on image. *Spring*, 1978:152–182.

———. 1979a. Image-sense. *Spring*, 1979:130–143.

———. 1979b. *The Dream and the Underworld*. New York: Harper and Row.

———. 1979c. Puer and Senex. In J. Hillman, et al., *Puer Papers*. Dallas: Spring Publications.

———. 1980. *Egalitarian Typologies Versus the Perception of the Unique*. Dallas: Spring Publications.

———. 1981. Silver and the white earth. *Spring*, 1981:21–66.

———. 1982. Salt: A chapter in alchemical psychology. In J. Stroud and G. Thomas, eds., *Images of the Untouched*. Dallas: Spring Publications.

Jacobi, J. 1973. *The Psychology of C. G. Jung*. New Haven, Conn.: Yale University Press.

Jarrett, J. 1981. Schopenhauer and Jung. *Spring*, 1981:193–204.

Joyce, J. 1961. *Ulysses*. New York: Vintage Books.

Jung, C. G. 1954. *The Symbolic Life: Miscellaneous Writings. CW*, vol. 18. Princeton, N.J.: Princeton University Press.

———. 1956. *Symbols of Transformation. CW*, vol. 5. Princeton, N.J.: Princeton University Press.

———. 1959. *Aion. CW*, vol. 9ii. Princeton, N.J.: Princeton University Press.

———. 1961. *Memories, Dreams, Reflections*. Recorded and edited by A. Jaffé. R. and C. Winston, trans. New York: Vintage.

———. 1963. *Mysterium Coniunctionis. CW*, vol. 14. Princeton, N.J.: Princeton University Press.

———. 1964. *Civilization in Transition. CW*, vol. 10. Princeton, N.J.: Princeton University Press.

———. 1966a. *The Practice of Psychotherapy. CW*, vol. 16. Princeton, N.J.: Princeton University Press.

———. 1966b. *Two Essays on Analytical Psychology. CW*, vol. 7. Princeton, N.J.: Princeton University Press.

———. 1967. *Alchemical Studies. CW*, vol. 13. Princeton, N.J.: Princeton University Press.

———. 1968a. *Archetypes and the Collective Unconscious. CW*, vol. 9i. Princeton, N.J.: Princeton University Press.

———. 1968b. *Psychology and Alchemy. CW*, vol. 12. Princeton, N.J.: Princeton University Press.

———. 1969a. *Psychology and Religion. CW*, vol. 11. Princeton, N.J.: University of Princeton Press.

———. 1969b. *The Structure and Dynamics of the Psyche. CW*, vol. 8. Princeton, N.J.: Princeton University Press.

———. 1970. *Civilization in Transition. CW*, vol. 10. Princeton, N.J.: Princeton University Press.

———. 1971. *Psychological Types. CW*, vol. 6. Princeton, N.J.: Princeton University Press.

———. 1973. *Letters*, vol. 1. G. Adler, ed. R. F. C. Hull, trans. Princeton, N.J.: Princeton University Press.

———. 1976. *The Visions Seminars: From the Complete Notes of Mary Foote*, vols. 1 and 2. Zurich: Spring Publications.

———. 1983. *The Zofinga Lectures. CW*, supp. vol. A. Princeton, N.J.: Princeton University Press.

———. 1985. *Freud and Psychoanalysis. CW*, vol. 4. Princeton, N.J.: Princeton University Press.

Kalsched, D. 1981. Limbo and the lost soul in psychotherapy. *Union Seminary Quarterly Review* 36, no. 2–3:95–107.

Kerenyi, K. 1977. Mnemosyne-Lesmosyne: On the springs of 'memory' and 'forgetting'. *Spring*, 1977:120–130.

Kerr, J. 1993. *A Most Dangerous Method*. New York: Knopf.

Kimball, J. 1997. *Odyssey of the Psyche: Jungian Patterns in Joyce's Ulysses*. Carbondale, Ill.: Southern Illinois University Press.

Kolve, V. A. 1984. The fool as killer of Christ in medieval art and literature. Unpublished lecture given at the University of Dallas, Irving, Texas.

Kugler, Paul. 1987. Childhood seduction: Physical and emotional. *Spring*, 1987:40–60.

Kuhn, T. S. 1962. *The Structure of Scientific Revolutions*. Chicago: University of Chicago Press.

Lawrence, D. H. 1976. *The Rainbow*. New York: Penguin Books.

Lingis, A. 1983. *Excesses: Eros and Culture.* Albany, N.Y.: State University of New York.

Lockhart, R. 1983. *Words as Eggs.* Dallas: Spring Publications.

Mallarmé, S. 1982a. *Stéphane Mallarmé: Selected Poetry and Prose.* B. Coffey, trans. M. A. Caws, ed. New York: New Directions.

Mazzotta, G. 1979. *Dante, Poet of the Desert: History and Allegory in the Divine Comedy.* Princeton, N.J.: Princeton University Press.

McGuire, W., ed. 1984. *Dream Analysis: Notes on the Seminar Given in 1928–1930 by C. G. Jung.* Princeton, N.J.: Princeton University Press.

McLynn, F. 1996. *Carl Gustav Jung.* New York: St. Martin's Press.

Megill, A. 1985. *Prophets of Doom.* Berkeley, Calif.: University of California Press.

Merleau-Ponty, M. 1962. *The Phenomenology of Perception.* C. Smith, trans. New Jersey: The Humanities Press.

———. 1963. *The Structure of Behavior.* A. Fisher, trans. Boston: Beacon Press.

———. 1968. *The Visible and the Invisible.* A. Lingis, trans. Evanston, Ill.: Northwestern University Press.

———. 1973. *The Prose of the World.* J. O'Neill, trans. Evanston, Ill.: Northwestern University Press.

Miller, D. 1973. *Gods and Games: Towards a Theology of Play.* New York: Harper and Row.

———. 1980. Theology's ego/religion's soul. *Spring,* 1980:78–88.

———. 1981. *Christs: Meditations on Archetypal Images in Christian Theology.* New York: The Seabury Press.

———. 1991. Angels, ghosts, and dreams: The dreams of religion and the religion of dreams. *The Journal of Pastoral Counseling* 26:18–28.

Mishima, Y. 1970. *Sun and Steel.* J. Besser, trans. New York: Grove Press.

Murray, G. 1963. Excursus on the ritual forms preserved in Greek tragedy. In J. Harrison, ed., *Themis.* London: Merlin Press.

Noll, R. 1994. *The Jung Cult: The Origins of a Charismatic Movement.* Princeton, N.J.: Princeton University Press.

Otto, R. 1923. *The Idea of the Holy.* London: Oxford University Press.

Otto, W. 1979. *The Homeric Gods: The Spiritual Significance of Greek Religion.* London: Pantheon Books.

Perls, F. 1971. *Gestalt Therapy Verbatim.* New York: Bantam.

Plato. 1961. *The Collected Dialogus of Plato.* E. Hamilton and H. Cairns, eds. Princeton, N.J.: Princeton University Press.

Polanyi, M. 1958. *Personal Knowledge: Towards a Post-Critical Philosophy.* Chicago: University of Chicago Press.

Portmann, A. 1964. *New Paths in Biology.* New York: Harper and Row.

———. 1967. *Animal Forms and Patterns.* New York: Shocken Books.

Rank, O. 1909. The myth of the birth of the hero. In Sigmund Freud, ed., *Schriften zur angewandten Seelenkunde,* no. 5. Leipzig.

Ricoeur, P. 1970. *Freud and Philosophy: An Essay in Interpretation.* D. Savage, trans. New Haven, Conn.: Yale University Press.

Riklin, F. 1907. Wish fulfillment and symbolism in fairy tales. In Sigmund Freud, ed., *Schriften zur angewandten Seelekunde,* no. 2. Leipzig.

Rilke, R. M. 1939. *Duino Elegies.* J. B. Leishman and S. Spender, trans. New York: Norton.

Rimbaud, A. 1966. *Rimbaud: Complete Works, Selected Letters.* W. Fowlie, trans. Chicago: University of Chicago Press.

Riquelme, J. P. 1991. *Harmony of Dissonance: T. S. Eliot, Romanticism, and Imagination.* Baltimore: John Hopkins University Press.

Rutter, P. 1991. *Sex in the Forbidden Zone.* New York: Fawcett Crest.

Samuels, A. 1985. *Jung and the Post-Jungians.* London: Routledge and Kegan Paul.

———. 1989. Beyond the feminine principle. In *The Plural Psyche.* New York: Routledge.

Satinover, J. 1985. At the mercy of another: Abandonment and restitution in psychosis and psychotic character. In N. Schwartz-Salant and M. Stein, eds., *Chiron 1985: Abandonment.* Wilmette, Ill.: Chiron Publications.

Schwartz-Salant, N. 1984. Archetypal factors underlying sexual acting out in the transference/countertransference process. In

N. Schwartz-Salant and M. Stein, eds., *Transference/ Countertransference*. Wilmette, Ill.: Chiron Publications.

_____. 1989. *The Borderline Personality: Vision and Healing*. Wilmette, Ill.: Chiron Publications.

Scott, C. 1982. *Boundaries in Mind*. New York: Crossroads.

Sheldrake, R. 1989. *The Presence of the Past: Morphic Resonance and the Habits of Nature*. New York: Vintage.

Smith, R. 1996. *The Wounded Jung*. Evanston, Ill.: Northwestern University Press.

Springer, A. 1995. Paying homage to the power of love. *The Journal of Analytical Psychology* 40, no. 1:41–58.

Stern, P. 1976. *C. G. Jung: The Haunted Prophet*. Evanston, Ill.: Northwestern University Press.

Stevens, W. 1947. *Poems*. New York: Vintage.

von Franz, M.-L. 1970. *C. G. Jung: His Myth in Our Time*. New York: Putnam.

Waite, A., ed. 1976. *The Hermetic and Alchemical Writings of Paracelsus*, vol. 1. Berkeley, Calif.: Shambala Press.

Watkins, M. 1984. *Waking Dreams*. Dallas: Spring.

Weston, J. 1957. *From Ritual to Romance*. Garden City, N.Y.: Doubleday.

Wheelwright, P. 1964. *Heraclitus*. New York: Atheneum.

Wilder, A. 1976. *Theopoetic: Theology and Religious Imagination*. Philadelphia: Fortress Press.

Winnicott, D. W. 1964. Memories, dreams, reflections. *International Journal of Psycho-analysis* 45:450–455.

_____. 1965. *The Maturational Process and the Facilitating Environment*. New York: International Universities Press.

Ziegler, A. 1983. *Archetypal Medicine*. G. Hartman, trans. Dallas: Spring Publications.

INDEX